Routledge Revivals

I0110163

Qur'an and Bible

Rival 'communities of the faithful' are not in the habit of reading each other's books, and when they do so, it is often to find fault and disparage. This attitude, so common a generation ago, is today giving way to mutual tolerance and an interest in 'dialogue'. However, we are still at the stage of being content with a superficial reading of each other's scriptures.

First published in 1978, *Qur'an and Bible* attempts to delve deeper, to solve some persistent puzzles, and to explore the common culture from which the Holy Books spring. Hebrew and Arabic, the original languages of the Bible and Qur'an are of the same linguistic family. Hence Arabic is a useful instrument with which to probe for the meaning of ancient Hebrew expressions and ideas as found in the Old Testament, and which continue to pose problems for translators and commentators. It is not merely a matter of one language elucidating another, but, more profoundly, of the light a language with a long unbroken tradition can throw on the desert culture shared by both the ancient Hebrews and the ancient Arabians.

Qur'an and Bible

Studies in Interpretation and Dialogue

M. S. Seale

Routledge
Taylor & Francis Group

First published in 1978
by Croom Helm Ltd

This edition first published in 2024 by Routledge
4 Park Square, Milton Park, Abingdon, Oxon, OX14 4RN

and by Routledge
605 Third Avenue, New York, NY 10017

Routledge is an imprint of the Taylor & Francis Group, an informa business

© 1978 M. S. Seale

All rights reserved. No part of this book may be reprinted or reproduced or utilised in any form or by any electronic, mechanical, or other means, now known or hereafter invented, including photocopying and recording, or in any information storage or retrieval system, without permission in writing from the publishers.

Publisher's Note
The publisher has gone to great lengths to ensure the quality of this reprint but points out that some imperfections in the original copies may be apparent.

Disclaimer
The publisher has made every effort to trace copyright holders and welcomes correspondence from those they have been unable to contact.

A Library of Congress record exists under LCCN: 79303641

ISBN: 978-1-032-94695-5 (hbk)
ISBN: 978-1-003-58127-7 (ebk)
ISBN: 978-1-032-94697-9 (pbk)

Book DOI 10.4324/9781003581277

Qur'an and Bible

STUDIES IN INTERPRETATION AND DIALOGUE·

M.S. SEALE

CROOM HELM LONDON

© 1978 M.S. Seale
Croom Helm Ltd, 2-10 St John's Road, London SW 11

British Library Cataloguing in Publication Data
Seale, Morris S.
    Qur'an and Bible.
    1. Koran — Relation to the Bible — Collected works
    I. Title
    297'.122   BP134.B4
    ISBN 0-85664-818-3

Printed and bound in Great Britain by
REDWOOD BURN LIMITED
Trowbridge & Esher

CONTENTS

ACKNOWLEDGEMENTS

Some of the ideas in the essay on 'The Mysterious Letters of the Qur an' were first presented in a paper I delivered to the International Congress of Orientalists in 1960.

A short version of my commentary on Judges 5 appeared in the *Journal of Biblical Literature,* vol. LXXXI, Part IV, 1962, under the title of 'Deborah's Ode and the Ancient Arabian Qasida'.

My translation of the Dialogue between a Saracen and a Christian, by John of Damascus, first appeared in the *Near East School of Theology Quarterly,* January and April 1973, Vol. 20, Nos. 1–2.

'The Ethics of Malamatiya Sufism and the Sermon on the Mount' first appeared in the *Muslim World,* Vol. LVIII, No. 1, 1968.

An Arab's Concern with Life After Death first appeared in *Life After Death* by Arnold Toynbee, Arthur Koestler and others, Weidenfeld and Nicolson, 1976.

'The Glosses in the Book of Genesis and the J E Theory' first appeared in *The Expository Times.*

'The Short Notes' appeared as editorials in the *Muslim World* in the period from April 1964 to January 1967.

Note on transliteration

No attempt has been made to adopt a systematic system of transliteration of Arabic words. In particular, diacritical marks have been omitted not to confuse the non-specialist. In the word 'Qur'an' which occurs frequently through the text the apostrophe which indicates the glottal stop should properly look left rather than right.

FOREWORD

What unites the essays in this book is the conviction of the interdependence of the Bible and the Qur'an, the sacred texts of three of the world's great religions. Rival 'communities of the faithful' are not in the habit of reading each other's books. When they do so, it is often to find fault and disparage. This attitude, so common a generation ago, is today giving way to a mutual tolerance and interest in 'dialogue'. However, we are still at the stage of being content with a superficial reading of each other's scriptures.

These essays are a modest attempt to delve a little deeper, to solve some persistent puzzles, and generally to explore the common culture from which the Holy Books spring. This work is meant not only for scholars, but for anyone interested in the language, origins and ideas of these ancient texts.

Hebrew and Arabic, the original languages of the Bible and the Qur an, are cognate, that is to say of the same linguistic family. I have found that Arabic, as used by the ancient Arabians some 1,500 years ago, is a useful instrument with which to probe for the meaning of ancient Hebrew expressions and ideas as found in the Old Testament and which continue to pose problems for translators and commentators. The usefulness of Arabic has, of course, long been recognised, but not, in my opinion, put to full use. It is not merely a matter of one language elucidating another, but, more profoundly, of the light a language with a long unbroken tradition can throw on the desert culture shared by both the ancient Hebrews and the ancient Arabians.

My hope is that these explorations will help build bridges of understanding and respect between members of different faiths.

THE AUTHOR

Dr Morris Searle is an orientalist, teacher and missionary who has spent forty years in Syria and Lebanon. He has made a special study of Arabic and Islamics, Sufism, Hebrew and Old Testament literature, and related theological and philological subjects, He has been a visiting professor at the Hartford Seminary Foundation, Connecticut, and has edited the *Muslim World*. He is currently teaching at the Near East School of Theology, Beirut. His publications include *Muslim Theology: A Study of Origins with Reference to the Church Fathers* (Luzac, 1964); *A Grammar of Biblical Hebrew in Arabic* (Beirut, 1971); *The Desert Bible* (Weidenfeld and Nicolson, 1974); and a translation of the book of Amos into classical Arabic for the ecumenical Arabic Bible.

1 THE HUMAN PREDICAMENT IN PRE-ISLAMIC ARABIA

The age-long debate between the world of Islam and the other 'Peoples of the Book', Christians and Jews, has all too often focused on the Qur'an as a literary composition. Muslims held it up as a miracle of eloquence, a unique and inimitable work, while their opponents saw it as repetitive sermonising in which a multiplicity of promises and threats, descriptions of paradise and hellfire, overshadowed its moral content. In the dust raised by this argument contestants on both sides tended to pay little or no attention to the message of the book, to the values it upholds and the evil practices it denounces. This is the quintessence of the work which is surely of far greater importance than its wording or literary style. Eloquence, however grand, cannot vie in significance with the task of banishing barbarism and introducing a new code of conduct — the task which the Qur'an sets out to achieve.

What then was the old way of life in pre-Islamic Arabia which the Qur'an wished to change? The age which preceded the emergence of Islam is commonly known as the *Jahiliyya,* which was thought to mean 'the age of ignorance' (from the Arabic *jahl,* 'ignorance'). More recent scholarship, and particularly the work of Ignaz Goldziher, has shown that the word denotes savagery and the absence of social morality, rather than merely ignorance. *Jahl,* in this sense, has as its opposite not knowledge but mildness and moderation. The most striking aspect of the *Jahiliyya* is that it was an age in which men acted on the general principle that might was right. In such a lawless and pagan society, robbery, rape and murder were commonplace, anxiety all-prevalent and compassion non-existent. Raiding, feuding and inter-tribal rivalries, an unbroken cycle of acts of violence, constituted the only way of life these ancient Arabians knew.

Our information about this dark age comes mainly from the poetry of the period and from collections of proverbs, fables and riddles — the principal literary forms, oral rather than written, of nomadic Arabia before Islam. From these sources, and more particularly from the poets, we get an idealised portrait of a society exhibiting the full range of nomadic virtues summed up in the Arabic word *muruwwa.* Literally, it means 'manliness' from *mar'u,* 'a man' (cf. the Latin *virtus,* 'moral excellence', from *vir,* 'a man'), but it embraces all the 'knightly' quali-

13

ties of valour and pride, loyalty and generosity, chivalry and vindictive-
ness. At the very root of Arabian society lay the pride of race, contests
for honour, feuds between tribes — all situations demanding a display
of manly virtues. As the pre-Islamic proverb has it, *la dina illa bi7
muruwwati*, 'there is no religion but manliness'.

Poets in the *Jahiliyya* were men of immense prestige. They were the
wise men, the thinkers and the historians of the tribe. The emergence of
a poet in a tribal family was celebrated with dance and song. The poems
which were preserved and memorised recorded the triumphs of the clan
and helped shape its identity. However, some of the great poets were
also brigands, such as Shanfara who, before his death, was outlawed by
his own tribe. As a result, he was driven to take to the desert, with wild
beasts his only companions, and to suffer stoically the rigours of life as
a fugitive. *Sa'alik* is the Arabic name for the wretched vagabonds and
destitute outlaws so common in the *Jahiliyya*. These *sa'alik* were dis-
owned by their clan which thus washed its hands of responsibility for
their crimes. Otherwise, any member of the tribe might be attacked and
killed in revenge. With the guilt of blood on his head, the outlaw was
the pariah of tribal society and stripped of the protection of his kin, he
became a homeless pauper who had to fend for himself. Usually he had
no recourse but to become a brigand. Indeed, Arabic literature is particularly rich in tales of brigandage. The truth is that the *muruwwa* sung
by the poets represents the Beduin ideal rather than the Beduin reality.
Life in the desert was harsh, merciless and often short. Such was the
social context in which the Qur'an emerged (although in Arabian cities
such as Mecca, Medina and Taif, life must have been somewhat more
secure).

The Qur'an is itself a source of information about life in the
Jahiliyya, but one which has often been overlooked. It contains a hand-
ful of highly concise but scattered passages condemning the norms of
social life at the time. The much-vaunted poets themselves came in for
fierce criticism and their influence was dismissed as evil. The pagan Arabs
believed that poetic inspiration was the work of the *jinn*, to the extent
that poets were thought to do no more than mouth words supplied
them by such spirits. But the quranic comment on the poets is scathing:

Shall I tell you on whom the devils descend? They descend on
every lying sinner. They eagerly listen, but most of them are liars.
Poets are followed by none save erring men. Behold how aim-
lessly they rove in every valley, preaching what they never practise.
[S.26: 221-6, Dawood's translation]

What justification was there for such wholesale condemnation of the poets, particularly when we know that the Prophet Muhammad himself had a poet, Hassan ibn Tabit, in his entourage? We cannot be certain of the immediate cause or occasion for the quranic indictment quoted above. Speaking generally, however, it may be said that the Prophet rightly saw the poets as troublemakers, stirring up strife by their satirical tirades, inflaming passions by exalting one side and abusing the enemy. They were especially good at invective and vilification, and, as they were usually dependent on patronage, they tended at the same time to be shameless flatterers and sycophants.

Like the pagan, insecure society from which they sprang, the poets were also unrepentant hedonists, snatching their share of happiness where they could find it. Tarafa, one of the masters of sixth-century Arabian verse, succinctly expressed their self-indulgence in his *Mu'allaq:*

If it were not for three things youth loves,
 I would not care when I died.
Red wine, well mixed and frothy;
a war-horse, when summoned to the fray;
a girl to be closeted with on a wintry day.

Thus, by denouncing the poets, the Qur'an ran counter to the whole ethos of the society in which poets were venerated and their attitudes widely accepted. It affirmed, in contrast, that the values lauded in the poems were false and that a community which based its morality on such premises was corrupt. The pursuit of wine, women and 'loot' could not be accepted as man's prime objective. The world, the Qur'an says, was not created in sport (S. 21: 16).

There are two telling phrases in the Qur'an which between them sum up the serious flaws in the pre-Islamic society: one is *hukm al-jahiliyya* (S.5: 50-5), which may be rendered as the 'code of conduct in the age of ignorance', and the other is *hamiyyat al-jahiliyya* (S.48: 26), which may be translated as the 'fury of the age of ignorance'. No doubt the nomad's code of honour included valour and hospitality, but these phrases point to a darker side.

For one thing, the nomad tended to be inordinately proud, flying into a rage at the slightest derogatory word or gesture. His reactions in defence of his honour were reckless and violent, and satire was the weapon he feared most. This was one of the reasons for the admiration and fear poets inspired. The Arabic word which sums up this towering hubris is *'anafa*, meaning 'pride', 'self-esteem', 'haughtiness', derived from *'anf*, a 'nose'; and the most insulting thing a nomad could do to another was to rub his nose in the dust.

To survive in the desert, the nomad had at all times to display strength, forever defending his rights and his honour, never showing a hint of moderation or compromise which might be interpreted as weakness. Always on his mettle, he had to hate his enemies as stead-fastly as he cared for his kin. This unashamed lust for revenge derives from tribal life where a man had to be his own policeman, judge and executioner. Retaliation was a duty set above all others, serving as a regulatory principle in society. A nomad was forever planning and plotting to get even with his enemy. Indeed, the thirst for revenge is spoken of in Arabian literature as a fever or a burning thirst. The fever is abated and the thirst quenched only when the enemy is destroyed, or at least humiliated. It was a philosophy of kill or be killed, rob or be robbed.

The Qur'an prescribes quite different attitudes. In opposition to the nomad's excessive pride, it advises: 'Do not strut haughtily, for you will neither split open the earth, nor rise to be as high as the mountains' (S.17: 37-9, author's translation). As for the nomad's thirst for ven-geance, the Qur'an recommends moderation (even though we may not see it as such today). Instead of a 'life for an eye' — the excessive vengefulness of the nomad's code — it recommends: 'A life for a life, an eye for an eye, a nose for a nose, an ear for an ear, a tooth for a tooth, and a wound for a wound. But if a man charitably forbears from retaliation, his remission shall atone for him' (S.5: 45, Dawood's translation). In other words, not only would the Qur'an have the punishment fit the crime, it also preaches forbearance, without however going so far as to suggest turning the other cheek. As for the excesses of hedonism, the Qur'an warns that the day will come when men shall say: 'Alas, for our heedlessness!' (S.6: 31).

The circumstances of tribal life dictated that tribal support had to be automatic, irrespective of the merits of the case. One defended one's relations right or wrong, not only because the whole protection system depended on it, but also because the honour of the clan was at stake. To fail a clansman in his hour of need was a source of eternal disgrace. As the sixth-century Arabian warrior-poet, Durayd ibn Simma, writes:

I belong to Ghaziyya, and hers I remain;
if she is in the right, I go along with her;
I could do no less if she were in the wrong.

[ʿIqd, V, 169]

In Abu Tammam's *Hamasa* (I, 5) is to be found a strange complaint by a nomadic Arabian poet, Qurayt ibn Unayf. He had been raided and had lost his camels. If only, he laments, he had been a member of another tribe, rather than of his own good-for-nothing clan which repaid good for evil and friendship for treachery. What truly shocking behaviour! Solidarity with one's clan lay at the very heart of the desert code of conduct: it was the nomad's only source of support and therefore infinitely precious. Tribal solidarity was his insurance policy and title to life. Without it, without the threat of retaliation by his tribe, he could be robbed and killed with impunity. What the Arabians called *silat al-rahm*, the sacred 'bond of relationship', could make the difference between life and death.

It was this very bond which the Qur'an dared challenge. It will be recalled that when the Hebrews made a golden calf and worshipped it, Moses mobilised a force of Levites and ordered them to punish the idolaters. What is remarkable about the biblical account in Exodus 32: 27-9 is that Moses said: 'Each of you kill his brother, his friend, his neighbour' — an order which, by overriding the claims of kinship, ran counter to deep-seated tribal beliefs and practices. Likewise the Qur'an, relating the story of the golden calf, repeats Moses' prescription: 'Slay yourselves' (S.2: 54). This seemingly puzzling command becomes clear when it is seen as an order to kill the offending kith and kin. As such it, too, is a judgement on the excesses of tribal solidarity and is a revolutionary innovation in a tribal society.

Like Moses some 1,800 years before him, Muhammad faced the problem of persuading his nomads to abandon the solidarity of kin and tribe in favour of a wider allegiance to the community of the faithful. A year or two after his arrival in Medina, the starting point of the Muslim era, he embodied these ideas in a charter which, as Professor Alfred Guillaume puts it, 'shows how the brotherhood of Islam took precedence over all other ties and relationships, so that a believing father might have to slay an unbelieving son.'[1] In fact, Muhammad's *umma* or community included not only members of different tribes, but also Jews, foreigners and slaves who had allied themselves to him.

What, then, was the religion which Islam displaced? From the scanty evidence available, the religion of the *Jahiliyya* seems to have consisted of little more than a few meaningless rituals which could no longer have enjoyed much credibility. To that extent, Islam emerged in something of a religious vacuum and the Qur'an dismisses contemptuously contemporary religious practices: 'Their prayers at the Sacred

House are nothing but whistling and clapping of hands' (S.8 35 Dawood's translation). The Arabian pagans had no scriptures, no temple officials, no religious disciplines; their sacred places were trees or rocks, sometimes in the charge of a keeper equipped with divining arrows to help supplicants resolve their problems. The shafts would be shuffled: one arrow advised action, another inaction, a third enjoined one to wait and see.

Like some Canaanite places of worship, the pagan *Ka'aba* in Mecca contained sacred stones within its perimeter, including the now venerated 'Black Stone', as well as images of gods. According to Ibn Ishaq, an early biographer of the Prophet, stone worship originated with the sons of Ishmael, Abraham's grandsons. On leaving Arabia they are said to have taken with them a stone from their homeland which they circumambulated as Ishmael did the *Ka'aba*. This act of worship led, according to the legend, to the worship of other stones.

The idols in the *Ka'aba* were female deities claimed by the pagan Meccans to be daughters of Allah. This is a notion which the Qur'an treats derisively in such passages as: 'The pagans pray to females: they pray to a rebellious Satan' (S.4: 117); and also in the following verses:

Have you thought on Al-Lat and Al-Uzzah, and, thirdly, on Manat [names of pagan goddesses] ? Is He to have daughters and you sons? This is indeed an unfair distinction! They are but names which you and your fathers have invented: Allah has vested no authority in them.

[S.53: 19-23, Dawood's translation]

It is curious that the pre-Islamic Arabians worshipped goddesses in a society in which women were second-class citizens. Indeed, a not infrequent practice was the killing of female children at birth. The birth of a baby girl was thought to be a source of possible future dishonour, as she might be taken prisoner and enslaved. Alternatively, her father might fall in battle leaving the girl at the mercy of an unkind relative, itself a cause of humiliation. Yet another reason for destroying a female child was the sheer problem of having another mouth to feed.

The Qur'an graphically describes the dilemma of a father unfortunate enough to hear of the birth of a girl:

When one of them is told of the birth of a daughter, his face darkens and he is filled with anger. He avoids company because of the bad news. Should he keep the child in spite of the disgrace or bury it in the dust?

[S.16:58, author's translation]

Little wonder then that the Qur'an condemns infanticide:

> You shall not kill your children for fear of want. We will provide for them and for you. To kill them is a great sin. [S.17: 31, Dawood's translation]

Because of the harshness and insecurity of desert life, where no man could be certain that he would end the day alive, the great predicament of the *Jahiliyya* was anxiety. Life hung by a thread. The nomadic poets speak of time and chance as the blind enemies of man, cutting him down at random and eventually sweeping everything into oblivion. The nomadic, pagan idea that *Time* (Arabic, *dahr*) is the killer rather than *God*, who for the believer is the arbiter of life and death, has caused the Arabic word *dahri* to mean a sceptic or atheist. This determinism of the desert is well summed up in a verse by one of the greatest of the Arabian poets, Zuhayr ibn Abu Sulma:

> I see fate as a kick from a blind camel:
>   if it is a hit, you are dead;
>   if a miss, you live until you are senile.

We find the same pessimism in Tarafa's *Golden Ode*:

> I swear that we are all tethered beasts,
> with the end of the rope held fast by death.

To this anxiety-ridden society, where life was hard and full of danger, the Qur'an brought a measure of reassurance. More importantly, it provided a body of doctrine which included a belief in a life after death. When the Meccans asked, 'When we are turned to bones and dust, shall we be raised to life?' the answer was: 'He who created you first is able to create you anew.' What is more, like the Jews and the Christians before them, the Arabians could now pride themselves on having a holy book of their own.

Note

1. Alfred Guillaume, *Islam* (Penguin Books, 2nd edn, 1956) p. 41.

2 THE COMMON 'WISDOM TRADITION' SHARED BY THE ANCIENT HEBREWS AND THE DESERT-DWELLING ARABIANS

It is generally recognised by students of the Old Testament that the books of Proverbs, Job and Ecclesiastes, known collectively as 'wisdom literature', stand somewhat apart from the rest of the Bible. It is at once obvious that they do not belong to any of the main literary categories, whether to the legal prescriptions of the Pentateuch, the historical narratives, the outpourings of the prophets, or to the sacred writings such as the Book of Psalms. Not only is wisdom literature a distinct literary genre, but the tone and content of these books, largely worldly-wise advice for getting by in life with little or no reference to religion, poses a problem for those who would wish to connect these works with divine revelation. The puzzle with which scholars have wrestled is how to fit this wisdom literature into the grand schema of Hebrew religion. How do these detailed recommendations about social life and manners, often expressed in the form of pithy sayings, relate to such large themes as the choice of the Hebrews, their deliverance from Egypt, the ordering of their moral life by the Decalogue and the sealing of their alliance with God by the Covenant? Clearly, the problem is one of establishing the origins of Hebrew wisdom and of clarifying its connection both to Old Testament ethics and to Old Testament religion.

The premise underlying nineteenth-century Old Testament scholarship was that the 'wise men of Israel' were heirs to the morality of the Decalogue; that 'wisdom literature' was dependent on and derivative from prophetic revelation; that the epigrammatic guides to conduct found in the Book of Proverbs were a secondary and later development of Yahwism. Such was the explicit or implicit belief of scholars like H. Schultz, J. Wellhausen and B. Duhm. These assumptions, however, were soon challenged, notably by H. Gunkel with his theory of literary types. Wisdom teaching was a genre so distinctive as to be *sui generis*, and therefore not credibly derived from either Mosaic law or prophetic writings. Gunkel's hypothesis was that wisdom literature emanated from a special class of 'wise men' in Hebrew society whose task was to educate the sons of the rich, using brief didactic sayings such as are found in Proverbs, for example, as their form of instruction.

The find, and publication in translation in 1923, of the teachings of

an ancient Egyptian moralist, Amen-em-ope, opened up a new approach
to the subject, causing considerable excitement among Old Testament
scholars. The Egyptian's sayings, set down in a manual of instruction
of thirty chapters, were found to bear a striking similarity to Proverbs
22 and 23.

Exploring this parallelism, such scholars as H. Gressman in Germany
and W.O.E. Oesterley in Britain surmised that Israel's 'wisdom teaching'
was borrowed from the more advanced civilisation of Egypt. It was
only one further step to say that it was therefore international rather
than native in character; and that it was very likely connected with life
at a royal court and may have been the product of court schools or
derived in some other way from the requirements of state administration.

However, this line of thinking has of late been contested, with some
modern scholars turning once again to clan life in ancient Israel for the
origin of Hebrew wisdom. On this interpretation, 'wisdom literature',
far from being a late product of sophisticated courtly or otherwise
privileged life, was one of the earliest expressions of popular culture,
with its origins rooted in pre-history. Both E. Gerstenberger in his
study of the Decalogue and H.W. Wolff in his study of Amos drew
attention to the existence of such an older folk wisdom originating in
the life of the Hebrew clans as they pursued their simple lives in rural or
nomadic settings.

This is a fruitful line of approach which enjoys an attractive prima
facie credibility. It is the purpose of this essay to advance the discussion by producing supporting evidence, in so far as this is possible.
I will argue the view that the origins of Hebrew wisdom literature are
indeed to be sought in the early tribal nomadic way of life of the
clans rather than in their later sedentary or urban culture where they
were exposed to external influences. Folk wisdom was, in my view,
authentic, popular and indigenous, rather than mannered, élitist and
borrowed from foreign models.

Of these foreign models, the most frequently cited, as has been
mentioned, is the manual of moral and religious instruction by the
Egyptian official Amen-em-ope, set out in thirty chapters. Clearly,
this document bears a remarkable similarity to Proverbs 22-4 and, more
particularly, to Proverbs 22: 17 to 23: 11. But, as Professor Helmer
Ringgren has pointed out, it is by no means clear which served as a
model for the other. 'No one can deny,' he writes, 'that there is similarity [between the two texts] . . . But which of the two is the older?
Has the author of Proverbs utilised Amenemope or vice versa?'[1]

Advocates of the view that Proverbs borrowed from the Egyptian text point to the Hebrew word *sholishim* of Proverbs 22: 20 which they interpret as 'thirty sayings', drawing the parallel with the thirty chapters of Amen-em-ope. But in my view, the Hebrew word has been misinterpreted, and this piece of evidence at least does not hold water. Although the word was originally unvowelled, *sholishim* (with a long vowel in the first syllable) is the traditional reading. To amend it to *sh'loshim,* 'thirty', means taking a considerable liberty not so much with the text but with the traditional reading of it. Another serious objection to reading the word as *sh'loshim* is that in this way one would get the phrase, 'I have written to you thirty / ? / in advice and knowledge'. But there is no indication of what the number 'thirty' qualifies. Certainly there is no Hebrew word standing for 'sayings' in the text. 'Thirty' on its own does not make much sense.

In my view, a more fruitful approach is to take the word *sholishim* as it stands in the text and attempt to arrive at a more satisfactory explanation of it. I suggest that *sholishim* is the plural of *sholish* which, to judge from its use in Isaiah 40: 12, means a 'tierce' or 'measure of three'. From this base, it is reasonable to suppose that the plural form of the same word in Proverbs 22: 20 means 'measures of three' − but, in this context, of metrical units. It will be observed that the passage in Proverbs beginning at Chapter 22: 17, entitled *The Sayings of the Wise,* takes the form of couplets in which each hemistich consists of three words, units or stresses. I believe that it is to *this* metrical pattern that the writer was referring when he says, 'I have written to you *sholishim* . . .', in other words, 'I have set out for you advice and knowledge in measures of three' − i.e. in 3:3 metrical form.

This interpretation will also help clarify the puzzling passage in 1 Samuel 18: 6 where it is related that, after David defeated Goliath, the women of Israel came out, singing and dancing, to greet the triumphant King Saul, 'with drums, with joy and with *sholishim'.* This last, which has so perplexed translators, including the authors of the New English Bible, must surely refer to the three-beat metrical chants of the women. The song they intoned was: 'Saul slays thousands, David ten thousands.'

I would argue, therefore, that there is no reference to 'thirty sayings' in the Hebrew text of Proverbs − indeed, one would be hard put to find that number in the passage in question − and that on this score, if on no other, no proof of borrowing from the Egyptian can be adduced.

If Hebrew wisdom was not then of foreign origin, where did it come from? There is a clue in 1 Kings 4: 30 where it is said that Solomon's wisdom excelled not only that of the B'nei Qedem, the 'men of the east', but also that of the Egyptians. Who then were these 'men of the east' who are given pride of place, even before the Egyptians, in the text? They are mentioned in Genesis 29: 1 where it is related that Jacob, fleeing from his jealous brother, made his way to the safety of his maternal uncles in the land of the 'men of the east'. These are identified by Professor Martin Noth as nomadic tribesmen inhabiting the fringes of the Syrian-Arabian desert.[2] What the Bible text of 1 Kings 4: 30 states explicitly is that these nomadic 'men of the east' possessed a tradition of wisdom, an accumulated fund of intelligent behaviour, which could stand comparison with that of Solomon and with that of the sedentary civilization of Egypt.

These 'men of the east' were nomadic Aramean herdsmen, and it was with this community that the ancient Hebrews identified themselves. Abraham called them 'his own kindred' and their lands 'his own country' (Gen. 24: 4). It was among this community that both Isaac and Jacob found brides (Gen. 24: 10 and 29: 1-29). These tribes of the east are repeatedly contrasted with the sedentary Canaanites with whom the Hebrew patriarchal family refused to intermarry. The clearest indication of Hebrew origins is to be found in the solemn recital of faith enjoined on every Hebrew in Deuteronomy 26: 5 and which opens with the words: 'A wild Aramean was my father . . .'[3] It is therefore only reasonable to suppose that the Hebrews shared the desert culture of the Arameans to whom they were so closely related, a culture in which 'wisdom tradition' was a vital ingredient.

In nomadic tribal life, a *bon mot* uttered by an elder or wise man on some special occasion was remembered, treasured and frequently repeated − not just the *mot* itself but the occasion which gave rise to it. These pithy sayings, which semitic languages such as Arabic and Hebrew in all their conciseness are adept at producing, became repositories of the collective intelligence of the clan. Such, in my view, was the genesis of at least the secular parts of the Book of Proverbs. Whatever later additions, alterations or improvements were made to the original drafts so as to result in the text we know today, there can be little doubt that the raw material was the product of the early existence of the Hebrew clans, grazing their flocks on the desert fringes, forever moving their encampments from one water-hole to another, before the process of settling started. This nomadic life-style was to remain more or less unchanged for the inhabitants of the Arabian and Syrian deserts until the advent of the twentieth century. It is no accident, therefore, that the same cultural phenomenon should be found among the

Arabs. A late flowering of pre-Islamic poems, proverbs, fables and riddles gives expression to the same legacy of the desert. This theory about the origins of Hebrew wisdom does not exclude the possibility of later borrowings from the more advanced civilisations with which the ancient Hebrews came into contact, particularly from the time of Solomon onwards. Clearly, they must have learned a good deal from both Canaan and Egypt, but what seems to me even more certain is that their early nomadism left an indelible stamp on their language, literature and ways of life.

A philological point may be adduced in support of the evident parallelism between Hebrew and Arabic prudential wisdom. There is a line in Labid's *Golden Ode,* one of the glories of pre-Islamic literature, which runs, 'We spring from a stock whose elders laid down a code, and every tribe has its code and exemplar'. The word Labid uses for 'code' is *sunnah,* to indicate the nomad's way of wisdom, the secular code of the desert. Later, the same word took on religious significance, standing for the Islamic *sunnah* of the Qur'an and tradition.

Sunnah is derived from the verbal form *sanna* which is the equivalent of the cognate Hebrew *shinein,* found in Deuteronomy 6: 7, which the Authorised Version renders as: 'Thou shalt teach them diligently *(shinanta)* unto thy children'; and the New English Bible as : 'You shall repeat them to your sons.' My translation would run: 'You shall make them your sons' code of behaviour.' In just the same way as *sunnah* started as a secular code in Arabic and only later took on a religious dimension, so the Hebrew *torah* initially meant 'instruction' of any kind before it came to mean the divine precepts of Yahweh. Proverbs 1: 8 provides an example of its secular, down-to-earth use, to mean an injunction given by a parent to a child: 'Attend, my son, to your father's instruction and do not reject the teaching *(torah)* of your mother.' This mother's *torah* is a gentler form of advice in contrast to the father's instruction which, in the Hebrew, implies the threat of punishment if disobeyed.

It would be hard to find a culture, however primitive, which does not include in its literature proverbs, riddles and fables. These forms are often the first attempt at literary expression, the first stirrings of a cultural consciousness. It is as if men in society felt the need to formulate in concise and memorable form certain basic precepts about social life and manners. Such sayings of the race are lessons learned from life, orally transmitted from one generation to another, by a father to his son, by the wise men of a tribe, by poets, by a leader to his followers. Taken together, they form a sort of moral profile of a society, incorporating its values, attitudes, ideals and taboos. They are not a body of laws but rather a set of precepts, derived from experience, instructing men in how to avoid the pitfalls of life, how to curb the excesses of temperament and passion and live in reasonable harmony with their environment. When, with the passage of time, these pregnant sayings are collected, as for example in the Book of Proverbs, or in the many collections of early Arabian proverbs and fables, a literary genre is created — 'wisdom literature'.

There is much talk of riddles in both the Old Testament and Arabian literature. Posing and solving verbal puzzles appear to have played a considerable role in social discourse, and a man could prove himself wise or unwise, quick-witted or dull according to his skill at entrapping others with his own conundrums or unravelling theirs. A man of reputed wisdom would need to have at his command a store of proverbs, riddles, aphorisms. In delivering a judgement it was clearly an advantage if ones views could be put strikingly in a memorable phrase. Solomon, for example, is described in 1 Kings 4: 31-4 as 'wiser than any man' because: 'he uttered three thousand proverbs, and his songs numbered a thousand and five. He discoursed of trees, from the cedar of Lebanon down to the marjoram that grows out of the wall, of beasts and birds, of reptiles and fishes. Men of all races came to listen to the wisdom of Solomon, and from all the kings of the earth who had heard of his wisdom he received gifts.' This text should not be read as suggesting that Solomon was a botanist or zoologist, but rather that his epigrams bore the stamp of keen observation which enabled him to draw on vivid examples from animal and plant life familiar to his listeners.

Hearing of Solomon's fame, the Queen of Sheba came to test his intelligence with riddles (1 Kings 10). Both the Authorised Version and the New English Bible somewhat miss the point by saying that she asked him 'hard questions'. In fact, as the text continues, he matched her verbal jousts word for word and no puzzle she posed proved too abstruse for him to solve. After this mental tussle, 'there was no more spirit left in her'.

Riddles were not only a test of mental agility; they were a form of entertainment; a pedagogical device to enable the pupil to retain a lesson; a rhetorical way of expressing profound truths. Isaiah, for example, asks in riddle form: 'Who has gauged the waters in the palm of his hand? . . . Who has measured the soil of the earth in a bushel?' (Isa. 40: 12.) This is echoed in Proverbs 30: 4 (a passage which has not always been recognised as a set of riddles):

Who has ever gone up to heaven and come down again?
Who has cupped the wind in the hollow of his hands?
Who has bound up the waters in the fold of his garment?
Who has fixed the boundaries of the earth?
What is his name, or his son's name, if you know it?

The same literary genre, an expression of nomadic wisdom, is found in Arabian literature. Al-Maydani (in his great book of proverbs, *Majma' al-amthal*) tells the story of a man called Shana, who, on a journey, embarassed his travelling companion by propounding riddles which the other found completely mystifying. Shana began by asking: 'Shall I carry you, or will you carry me?' As they were both well-mounted, his companion, greatly puzzled, could find no adequate reply. Approaching a village, they saw a field being harvested, whereupon Shana asked his companion: 'Has the crop been already consumed, or is there something left over?' Once again his companion kept silent. They then caught up with a funeral procession which promoted Shana to pose another riddle: 'Is the man alive or dead?'

On arrival home, Shana's bemused companion told his daughter of his strange experience. However, she had no difficulty in answering all three puzzles. She explained that the question who was to carry whom meant which of them would entertain the other on the journey and so while away the tedium. The question about the harvested field was meant to elicit whether the poor farmer had already sold the crop and spent the proceeds or whether he still had some reserves in hand. As for the question about the corpse, it was meant to discover whether the dead man had left behind a male heir. When Shana was told the girl's answers to his riddles, he promptly asked for her hand in marriage.

The range and diversity of the subject-matter of Solomon's proverbs is matched in Arabian literature. There are Arabic proverbs relating to the wild ass roaming the desert heights and to the bug under the camel's hoof; to the eagle, the butterfly and the moth; to the *naba'* tree from whose branches the nomad cut the hard wood for his bow and arrows; to the low-lying colocynth, a medicinal herb which the nomad put to many uses. Compared to the wealth of animal proverbs in the Arabian collections, the Old Testament can offer only a modest number in Proverbs 30. For example, Proverbs 30: 28 reads: 'The lizard grasps with her hands and is found in the palaces of kings.' This is echoed by the Arabian proverb, a product of the same environment: 'A grasp more deadly than the lizard's.' Nomads, whether Hebrew or Arabian, were evidently struck by the way the lizard seized and devoured its offspring.

They also observed the lizard's ability to do without water, hence the Arabian proverb: 'More saturated than the lizard.'

The harsh primitiveness of desert life accounts for the coarseness of some of the sayings. Al-Bakri affirms that many of the stories behind the proverbs are too revolting to relate, but he relates them nonetheless.[4] Al-Maydani's *Majma' al-amthal* contains some entries which are somewhat more acceptable such as, 'He is crawling with lice', to mean 'He is very rich'. Others, taken at random, are: 'If one ass urinates, the others follow suit'; or 'Your son is the offspring of your genitals'; or — in this case a proverb reviling a desert deity — 'He is a vile god who has allowed himself to become a urinal for foxes.' Another betrays the true callousness of the desert: 'To lose an old barren female is no great calamity.'

The basic tone of much of the Book of Proverbs, like that of the Arabian sayings, is prudential rather than apodictic: a course of action, for example, might be warned against, not for religious or ethical reasons, not because God forbade it, but for fear of being found out. The warning in Proverbs 1: 10-19 to a young man not to fall in with a band of cut-throats and robbers is supported by the dangers of discovery. Similarly, the well-known passage of Proverbs 7: 6-23, warning against succumbing to the temptation of an adulteress, underlines not the immorality of the act but its dire consequences: 'Till a dart (thrown by the husband) strike through his liver . . .'

Yahweh does, of course, make his appearance in the Book of Proverbs, but, as R.B.Y. Scott has demonstrated in his definitive study, references to him are later additions to the secular substructure. As he puts it, 'those sayings which specially affirm Yahweh's active presence represent an annotation or editing of an already existing collection of wisdom couplets'. He says further 'that many sayings seem designed *either* to correct views expressed in other proverbs *or* to put them in a new light by adding a religious dimension'.[5] One or two examples from his work may suffice to illustrate the sort of editing that must have taken place: 'A rich man's wealth is his strong city' (Prov. 18: 11) is corrected by the preceding verse, 'The name of Yahweh is a strong tower'. Similarly, 'The teaching of the wise is a fountain of life' (Prov. 13: 4a) is emended in a later verse to read, 'The fear of Yahweh is a fountain of life' (Prov. 14: 27a).

As with the Hebrews, so with the Arabians. Secular proverbs, and the way of life they reflected, had to be emended to suit the dictates of the new religion. The coming of Islam imposed a new code of behaviour requiring new sayings, or at least a reinterpretation of old ones. Zuhayr ibn Abu Sulma's celebrated pre-Islamic saying, 'Whoever assaults not others will himself be assaulted', was reinterpreted by Muslims to mean, 'Assault in self-defence'. Or, to take another example, the well-known nomadic proverb, 'In war dupe your enemy', was changed into, 'On no account let your enemy dupe you, or you will be doomed'. Finally, the old Arabian nomadic prescription regarding tribal solidarity, 'Go to your brother's help, whether he be right or wrong', was reinterpreted by Islam to mean, 'If your brother does wrong, help him back on to the right path'.

I have tried in this essay to show that, for Hebrews and Arabians, wisdom literature was a product of the ancient desert culture which nurtured both. The similarities which their two literatures display in form, content and vocabulary provide evidence of their common origin. Both peoples encountered religion, gave up their early barbarity and changed their ways. Both, at different times, underwent a spiritual revolution which found expression in their everyday sayings. It is the common cultural heritage of the desert, rather than any piecemeal or wholesale borrowing from more civilised neighbours which, to my mind, holds the key to the understanding of their earliest sapiential tradition.

Notes

1. Helmer Ringgren, *Studies in the Religion of Ancient Israel*, p. 3.
2. Martin Noth, *1 Kings*, pp. 81-2.
3. For the translation of *obeid* as 'wild' see M.S. Searle, *The Desert Bible*, London 1974, p. 151.
4. Abu 'Ubeid al-Bakri, *Fasi al-maqal*, ed. Dr Ihsan Abbas (Beirut, 1971), pp. 502-5.
5. R.B.Y. Scott, *Studies in the Religion of Israel*, pp. 146-65.

3 THE MYSTERIOUS LETTERS OF THE QUR'AN

Introduction

> It is He who sent down upon thee the Book wherein are verses clear
> that are the Essence of the Book, and others ambiguous.
>
> [Qur'an 3: 7]

A claim the Qur'an makes repeatedly for the Revelation communicated
to Muhammad is that it is clear and wholly intelligible. The 'noble
book' is described as *kitab mubin,* meaning that it is explicit beyond
question. This is in fact true of a great part of this remarkable work
which provides an overall vision of God, man and nature. And yet it
must be said that there are some particulars in the text which are not
perfectly plain — an admission the Qur'an makes about itself. A great
master of Muslim learning of the Mamluk period, Jalal al-Din al-Suyuti,
expended a good deal of effort and ingenuity attempting to interpret
obscure and ambiguous passages, those described in the Qur'an as
mutashabihat.

Al-Suyuti's *Itqan,* an exhaustive survey of Quranic scholarship, includes a long chapter (section 43) devoted to an exploration of Quranic
ambiguities. Of these he lists several principal types. One, for example,
concerns human features and actions ascribed to God: the deity is
described as 'mounting a throne' or as 'possessing a face' or an 'eye' or
indeed a 'right hand'. But these attributes are clearly difficult to recon-
cile with the Islamic dogma of divine transcendence. On this very issue,
that of the ascription to God of human parts and passions, the orthodox battled with liberal innovators for centuries.

Another source of difficulty in the Qur'an relates to the so-called
'abrogated' and 'abrogating' verses. The problem here is that the Qur'an
relates that the Prophet is on some occasions told that parts of his
Revelation are to be erased and forgotten in order to be replaced by
better passages. However, as the book does not identify the verses
which are thus to be cancelled, commentators are presented with a
great source of puzzlement.

It is a third area of ambiguity dealt with by al-Suyuti and by generations of Islamic scholars which will principally occupy us. This concerns the unintelligible and unexplained single letters and groups of
letters which stand at the beginning of no fewer than twenty-nine

Suras. They are positioned after the traditional *basmala* (in the name of God, the Compassionate and the Merciful) and before the opening verse. Throughout the ages, scholars both Muslim and European, have pondered and wrestled with these mysterious letters, advancing a great number of theories, sometimes fanciful and far-fetched, to explain their origin and meaning. To the ultra-orthodox, their secret is known to God alone.

As will be seen from my translation in the second part of this essay, al-Suyuti reviews dozens of possible theories, many of them asserting that the letters are abbreviations of one or other of the ninety-nine names of God. On one such interpretation, for instance, attributed to Ibn Abbas, the five letters which head Sura 19 — *kaf ha ya 'ain sad* — stand respectively for *karim* (noble), *hadi* (guide), *hakim* (wise), *'alim* (knowing) and *sadiq* (truthful). The snag is that the *ya* which is said to stand for *hakim* is not the initial letter of this word but one chosen arbitrarily. Another version of the same tradition has it that *ya* stands for *amin* (faithful). Yet another, attributed to Ibn Mas'ud, one of the Prophet's companions, suggests that the *ya* stands for *'aziz* (mighty). The door is open to word-games which can be given little credibility.

Another school of interpretation attributes numerical values to the letters in such a way, for example, as to suggest that *alif lam mim*, the three letters which head Sura 2, stand respectively for the numerals 1, 30 and 40, making a total of 71. This was said by some to be the number of years the Prophet would rule — although, as al-Suyuti relates, the addition of further letters could indicate a longer spell of time, up to a grand total of no less than 704 years! No wonder the learned commentators scratched their heads in bewilderment. Hardly less forced was the suggestion of al-Huwayyi that the letters were used by Gabriel as a sort of signal to rouse Muhammad from his other activities and warn him of the approach of a revelation.

Among European scholars, A. Sprenger is the author of one of the strangest hypotheses: that the five letters heading Sura 19, the chapter entitled 'Mary' and which deals, among other subjects, with the miraculous birth of Jesus, constitute a mystical monogram, *'Isa al-Nasiri malik al-yahud,* an Arabic equivalent of *Iesus Nazarenus Rex Iudaeorum* (INRI). According to this view, *kaf* stands for *malik*, *ha* and *ya* for *yahud*, *'ain* for *'isa* and *sad* for *nasiri*. As will be seen, this involves some juggling with the letters, quite apart from the implausibility of the Qur'an quoting the Roman Governor Pilate's mocking inscription on the Cross.

Another explanation which has gained some currency among European scholars is that the letters are the initials of the persons who furnished Zaid ibn Thabit with Suras or fragments of Suras when he was commissioned by the Caliph to carry out the recension of the text. According to this theory, first advanced by Nöldeke, then repudiated by him but later revived by H. Hirschfield, the letters were marks indicating the ownership of the manuscript copies. To this day in the East, goods in transit, such as boxes of fruit and vegetables on their way to market, are marked with their owners' names. Such customs no doubt date back to the trans-desert trading caravans. In the same way, manuscripts on loan to Zaid might well have been marked with the owners' initials.

But there are at least two serious objections to this theory. The first is that the initial letters alone are of little use in tracing the alleged owners seeing that Arabic proliferates with names with the same initials. The second difficulty is that, while the letters sometimes occur singly, they are also found in groups of from two to five together. Is one to believe that there were two to five different owners of each manuscript or as many different copies of the same manuscript? There are puzzles here which make the theory difficult to accept.

Two scholars, Hans Bauer[1] and Eduard Goosens[2], come a step closer to a plausible solution of the problem. Their interpretations are discussed by Professor Arthur Jeffery in an article entitled 'The Mystic Letters of the Koran'.[3] The argument runs as follows: Seeing that some Suras take their names from the initial letters (Sura 20, for example, known as *ta ha;* Sura 36 known as *ya sin;* Sura 38 known as *sad;* and Sura 50 known as *qaf);* and seeing also that other Suras take their names from catch-words in the text (Sura 2, for example, known as 'The Cow', because of a striking passage in it about an injunction by Moses to sacrifice a red heifer); it may, therefore, be inferred that the letters which serve as titles are themselves abbreviations for some striking word in the Suras.

E. Goosens was led to believe that the letters were 'some sort of technical introduction to the Suras', perhaps 'the remains of old names which once were current'. This approach by both Bauer and Goosens is promising, although they themselves were not very successful in linking the introductory letters to anything significant in the Suras.

An Attempt at Cracking the Code of the Mysterious Letters

The significance of the mysterious initial letters of the Qur an has eluded believers and commentators from the first century to this day. Many attempts have been made to crack the code, and this essay must take its place as yet another, almost certainly imperfect, solution of a millennial puzzle.

The letters occur at the head of twenty-nine Suras singly (Suras 38, 50, 68), or in pairs (Suras 20, 27, 36, 40, 41, 43, 44, 45, 46), or in threes (Suras 10, 11, 12, 14, 15, and 26, 28, and 2, 3, 29, 30, 31, 32), or in fours (Suras 7, 13), or in fives (Suras 19, 42).

What follows is an explanatory analysis of each initial letter or groups of letters.

Sad (Sura 38)

The letter *sad* in Sura 38 not only stands alone before the first verse, but also gives its name to the Sura. I conjecture that it is an abbreviation for the noun *sala*, meaning 'hellfire', or, as a verb, 'to roast in hell'. *Vv.* 55-63 of this Sura speak graphically of the punishment of the damned — 'There let them taste their drink: scalding water, festering blood and other putrid things' — and probably formed the core of the Sura before it was expanded with the stories of David and Solomon. Significantly, one of the opening verses of the Sura — 'How many generations We have destroyed before them' — is a sort of refrain which is found also in the 'Hellfire' section of Sura 19. The introductory letter *sad*, therefore, appears to stand as a pointer of a sort of index to the contents of the Sura.

Qaf (Sura 50)

This Sura also takes its name from the letter *qaf* which stands along before the first verse. I conjecture that it stands for *qarin*, the 'companion' or *alter ego* of *vv.*23 and 27 who, the Qur'an says, both misleads the sinner and testifies against him. The Judgement Day scene in which this evil spirit makes his appearance is one of the most striking of the Sura. The introductory *qaf* thus appears to stand as a pointer to this central episode.

Nun (Sura 68)

The word *nun*, meaning 'fish', is rare in Arabic and was probably borrowed from Aramaic or Syriac. it is found in Sura 21: 87 where Jonah is referred to as *Dhu-al-nun*, the 'man of the fish'. Sura 68, headed by the letter *nun*, also contains a brief reference to Jonah (' . . . be not like him of the fish, who cried out in despair . . . ' *v.* 48), but, interestingly enough, the word used in the text for fish is not *nun*, but the more common *hut*. I conjecture, nevertheless, that the introductory *nun* stands as a pointer to the reference to Jonah in the Sura — once again a brief guide to the contents.

Ta Ha (Sura 20)

These two Arabic letters, standing before the first verse of Sura 20, also give their name to the Sura which is principally concerned with the story of Moses. My suggestion is that *ta* stands for *Tuwa*, the sacred valley where Moses first entered the presence of God (v. 12). *Ha*, in turn, stands for *Harun*, Aron, the brother of Moses, who is rebuked for his part in making the golden calf an object of pagan worship. Clearly, *Tuwa* and *Harun* are two key proper names occurring in the Sura. They are, as it were, picked out for special prominence by the introductory letters.

Ta sin (Sura 27)

Sura 27 is largely concerned with birds. It relates that Solomon, on succeeding David, made the following declaration to his people in which, as will be seen, birds figure largely:

> Know, my people: we have been taught the tongue of birds (v. 16). He then marshalled his forces, of Jinn, men and birds and set them in battle array (v. 17). He then inspected his birds and said, 'Where is the Hoopoe? I cannot see him here . . .' (v. 20)

It emerges later that the bird had been on a mission to the Queen of Sheba and returned to report to Solomon on life at her court. Solomon then sent the bird back with a message for the Queen (v. 28).

Clearly, birds and in particular the remarkable hoopoe (Arabic, *hudhud*) are among the most striking personages in the Sura and I therefore conjecture that *ta sin* stands for *tair Sulaiman*, 'Solomon's birds'. Once again, the introductory letters are a pointer to the principal contents. This Sura is, in fact, called 'The Ant' but this insect is only referred to briefly (v. 18) and enjoys nothing like the prominence given to the birds.

Ya sin (Sura 36)

These two initial letters also give their names to Sura 36. In interpreting them, my argument rests on the opinion that this Sura and the next, Sura 37, were originally one chapter. Indeed, they share a common rhyme (except for the first eleven verses of Sura 37, a fragment with a different rhyme which does not connect with the rest). They also share a common theme, a defence of life after death made by the Prophet in rebuttal of the scepticism of the Meccans. 'Who will give life to rotten bones?' asks the sceptic (S. 36: 78). The answer follows: 'He who created them at first will give them life again' (S. 36: 79).

The very same exchange is found in Sura 37: 'When we are dead and turned to dust and bones, shall we be raised to life . . .?' (S. 37: 17). Answered by, 'Yes. And you shall be held to shame' (S. 37: 18).

Goosens has also suggested that these two Suras were once joined together, although his interpretation of *ya sin* as a reference to the prophet Eliasin (S. 37: 130) is unconvincing because this prophet enjoys a mere mention and plays no role whatsoever in the narrative.

My contention, however, is that, seeing that Sura 37 does contain the fullest account found in the Qur'an of the story of Jonah (vv. 139-48), the introductory letters *ya sin* which stand at the beginning of Sura 36 stand for *Yunus,* Arabic for Jonah, and were the old title of the two Suras conjoined. One must presume that an editor mistakenly divided the Suras, inserted the fragment which now forms the first eleven verses of Sura 37, and gave the title of Jonah to Sura 10 which contains a mere mention of the prophet (v. 99) without saying anything about him. I conclude, therefore, that *ya sin* must be read as a sort of secret pointer to the full story of Jonah in Sura 37.

Ta sin mim (Suras 26, 28)

Suras 26 and 28 are complementary, the first narrating the career of Moses from his call, the second recounting his birth and early life. I conjecture that *ta sin mim* stands for *tur sina musa,* that is to say, 'Mount Sinai' and 'Moses', names which point to the principal contents of these Suras. A reference to the Mount *(tur)* is found twice in Sura 28 (vv. 44 and 46). Mount Sinai and its significance as the place where Moses received the law must have been familiar to Muhammad and there are two other references to it in the Qur'an (S. 23: 20 and 95: 2).

Kaf ha ya 'ain sad (Sura 19)

In my view, this group of five letters standing at the beginning of the important Sura entitled 'Mary', where the births of both John the Baptist and Jesus are recounted, provides the most convincing evidence that these mysterious letters are mnemonics — an insider's guide to the Sura's contents.

Five personages or elements are introduced in the Sura in the following order: the priest, Zacharia; the temple where he had his vision; the birth of John; Jesus, the son of Mary; and finally Abraham, a 'man of truth' (heading a list of other prophets). I suggest that the introductory letters are a guide to these contents. *Kaf,* in my view, stands for *kahin,* used here in the Hebrew sense of a 'priest', rather than in the

Arabic sense of a 'sorcerer'. (It may be said here in parentheses that there are several instances in the Qur'an of the use of Hebrew words. For example, the Ark is described in Sura 2: 248 as containing the Lord's *sakina*. The Arabic means 'calm' or 'tranquillity', whereas the Hebrew *shekhina,* meaning 'Divine presence', is evidently closer to the intended sense. Similarly, the use of *ahad* in Sura 112, rather than the more usual *wahid,* to indicate the unity of God, echoes the Hebrew *aehad* of Deuteronomy 6: 4 — 'Hear, O Israel, Yahweh our God, is *one* Lord.')

We move next to *ha* which, in my view, stands for *haikal,* the 'temple' where Zacharia had his vision. This word, however, is not to be found in the text of the Sura where *mihrab,* a niche in a temple, is used instead.

Ya stands for *Yahya,* John the Baptist; *'ain* stands for *'Isa,* 'Jesus'; and finally, the letter *sad* stands for *siddiq,* the 'man of truth', the appellation given to Abraham. The five initial letters are thus seen to be a *memoria technica* of the Sura's contents.

Alif lam ra (Suras 10, 11, 12, 14, 15)

This group of five Suras deals with the general subject of prophets and prophecy, and indeed all but Sura 15 are named after prophets: Jonah, Hud (a non-biblical, Arabian prophet), Joseph and Abraham. In my view, *alif lam ra* stands for the word *al-rusul,* meaning God's messengers, the prophets. In this case, the introductory letters are a mnemonic for a general topic or theme.

Alif lam mim (Suras 2, 3, 29, 30, 31, 32)

This second large group of Suras introduced by letters is more concerned with exhortation than with history, although it draws lessons from history and enlivens its teaching with an occasional parable. It also includes legislation. Here, I conjecture, the introductory letters *alif lam mim* stand for *al-mau'iza,* meaning 'instruction', 'edification' or 'sermonising'. This is how the Qur'an and other Scriptures are often described in the Qur'an itself (2: 66 and 275; 3: 138; 5: 46; 7: 145; 10: 57; 11: 120; 16: 125; 24: 34).

Alif lam mim sad (Sura 7)

As the first three letters suggest, this Sura is one of the just mentioned *al-mau'iza* group, but with the addition of *sad* which, as we saw with Sura 38 above, I take to stand for 'hellfire' or 'to roast in hell'. This, then, is a Sura which is principally concerned with drawing edifying lessons from the story of Moses and from other episodes in Biblical and Arabian prophetic history — but with a central passage, vv. 38-51, dealing with the torments of hell suffered by the 'dwellers of the fire'.

Alif lam mim ra (Sura 13)

This Sura is another member of the *al-mau'iza* group. Its principal theme is that the elements, thunder, lightning and flood, are Allah's parables, teaching men to distinguish between good and evil, and to understand their consequences, reward and punishment. The addition of *ra* to the three initial letters is meant to signify *ra'd*, 'thunder', a word which occurs in v. 13 ('The thunder sounds his praise . . .') and which is indeed the central idea of the Sura, providing its title.

Ha mim (Suras 40, 41, 43, 44, 45, 46) Ha mim 'ain sin qaf (Sura 42)

These seven short, amorphous Suras, more like fragments of chapters than complete works, form a puzzling group. My theory is that they are unfinished compositions which the Prophet laid aside in the hope of being able to add to them such embellishments, parables or snatches of history as later inspiration might provide. On this argument, *ha mim* might stand for the Arabic *hadith muqatta*, 'unfinished narrative', indicating that they required further work.

As for the three additional letters of Sura 42, *'ain sin qaf*, I take them to be a reminder that this material should be 'added to similar rhymed prose'. This interpretation is arrived at as follows: *Sag'a* in Arabic means 'rhymed prose'; *Qarina* means 'joined', 'associated' or 'similar'; *Ind* is a preposition meaning 'at', 'near' or 'beside'. So I take *'ain sin qaf* to stand for *'ind sag'a qarina*,[4] meaning 'to be set beside material rhyming in the same way'. The introductory letters of Sura 42 should therefore be read as a note suggesting that this was an incomplete fragment to be expanded in due course when suitably rhymed material became available. I like to believe that this interpretation finds some support in a view put forward by Professor Jeffery:

> Recent research of Dr Bell of Edinburgh and Professor Torrey of Yale has suggested that there is internal evidence in the Quran itself that the Prophet kept in his own care a considerable mass of revelation material belonging to various periods of his activity, some of it in revised and some of it in unrevised form, and that this material was to form the basis of the *kitab* he wished to give his community before he died. Death, however, overtook him before anything was done about this matter.[5]

Conclusion

It is the thesis of this essay that the standing puzzle posed to Islamic scholarship by the initial letters found at the beginning of twenty-nine Suras may be explained by reading them as mnemonics or as abbreviated tables of contents.

They appear to be of three related types: (a) pointers to central or striking passages in the Suras, such as *sad* in Sura 38 standing for 'hellfire'; (b) indications of the general nature of groups of Suras, such as the *al-rusul* group or the *al-mau'iza* group, dealing respectively with prophecy and homiletics; (c) notes to remind the author or editor that the material was in an unfinished state, such as the *ha mim* group.

Clearly, such pointers or mnemonics would have been of great usefulness to the *qurra*', the Qur'an readers, or to the later *huffaz*, those who committed the Book to memory, not to mention the *imam*, who led the public worship. The letters would not only help locate passages, but would also, in some cases, as in Sura 19, indicate the order in which the various personages and ideas appeared. In dealing with a skeleton text, lacking both vowels and diacritical marks, any such guide to the contents would be welcome.

If these letters were so useful, why was their significance forgotten from very early times? Were they, perhaps, a sort of secret index known only to an elite and dying with it? The fact that some of the introductory letters are still used as the titles of certain Suras, such as *ta ha* of Sura 20, suggests that these letters ante-date some of the other titles given to the Suras. These tend either to be the opening word of a Sura (such as Sura 37, 'The Ranks'), or a catch-word taken from the body of the text (such as Sura 2, 'The Cow'). In any event, it would appear that the naming of the Suras was the work of compilers after Muhammad's death and that this work was never finalised. Indeed, this uncertainty about naming may be illustrated by Sura 9 which is headed 'Repentance or Immunity or other names by which it is known'.

Al-Suyuti's Review of Past Attempts

A Translation of the passage on the Initial Letters of the Suras in *al-Itqan fi 'ulum al-Qur'an* by Jalal al-Din al-Suyuti

> Jalal al-Din al-Suyuti was the most prolific Egyptian writer in the Mamluk period and perhaps in Arabic literature. He was born in Cairo in 1445 (849) and died in 1505 (911). The very long list of

his writings compiled by Flugel in the *Wiener Jahrbuch*, 1832, vols. 58-60, gives 561 works, but it includes numerous quite short treatises. His ambition was to try his skill in all branches of Muslim learning. His *Itqan*, from which the translation below is made, is the most exhaustive presentation of all branches of study relating to the Qur'an. [Arabic text edited by Muhammed Abu al-Fadl Ibrahim, Cairo, 1967. the translation is of pp. 21-30 from Vol. 3-4]

Among the ambiguities [in the Qur'an] are the initial letters of the Suras, and the preferred view about them is that they are among the secrets known only to God, may He be exalted.

A tradition by Ibn al-Mundhir and others reported that al-Sha'bi, when questioned about the initial letters, said: Every book holds a secret, and the secret of the Qur'an is the initial letters.

A tradition by Ibn Abu Hatim and others, by way of Abu Duha, reported Ibn Abbas as saying that *alif lam mim* stand for 'I am the knowing God'; *alif lam mim sad* for 'I am the deciding God', and *alif lam ra* for 'I am the seeing God'.

A tradition by Sa'id ibn Jubair reported Ibn Ibbas as saying: *alif lam mim, ha mim* and *nun* are fragments of names. A tradition by way of Ibn Ikrama reported Ibn Abbas as saying that *alif lam ra, ha mim* and *nun* are disjointed letters standing for *al-Rahman* (the Merciful).

A tradition by Abu'l Shaikh reported Muhammad ibn Ka'b al-Karazi as saying that *alif lam ra* are from the name *al-Rahman*. He also said that in *alif lam mim sad, alif* stands for Allah, *mim* for al-Rahman, and *sad* for al-Samad (the Eternal).

A tradition reported al-Dahhak as saying that *alif lam mim sad* stand for 'I am the truthful God'; and two other interpretations by al-Karmani in his *Ghara 'ib* are that *alif lam mim sad* are said to stand for 'I am God the Creator' and that *alif lam ra* are said to stand for 'I am the Knowing and the Exalted God'.

A tradition by al-Hakim and others, by way of Sa'id ibn Jubair, reported Ibn Abbas as saying that in *kaf ha ya 'ain sad, kaf* stands for *karim* (noble); *ha* for *hadi* (guide); *ya* for *hakim* (wise); *'ain* for *'alim* (omniscient); *sad* for *sadiq* (truthful).

A tradition also by al-Hakim from another point of view reported Said ibn Abbas as saying that *kaf ha ya 'ain sad* stands for *kafi* (all-sufficient), *hadi* (guide), *amin* (faithful), *'aziz* (mighty) and *sadiq* (truthful).

A tradition by Ibn Abu Hatim, by way of Suddi from Abu Malik and Abu Salih reported Ibn Abbas and Ibn Mas'ud and Murrah and some

of the Prophet's companions as saying that *kaf ha ya 'ain sad* are fragments in which *kaf* stands for *al-malik* (the king), *ha* for Allah, *ya* and
'ain for *'aziz* (Mighty) and *sad* for *al-Musawwir* (the Creator).

A similar tradition was reported from Muhammad ibn Ka'b, save
that he said that *sad* stands for *al-Samad* (the Eternal).

From another point of view, a tradition by Sa'id ibn Mansur and Ibn
Mardaway reported Said ibn Abbas as saying that *kaf ha ya 'ain sad*
stands for *Kabir* (great), *hadi* (guide), *amin* (faithful), *'aziz* (mighty),
sadiq (truthful).

A tradition by Ibn Mardaway, by way of al-Kalbi from Abu Salih
reported Ibn Abbas as saying that the letters stand for *al-kafi* (the all-
sufficient); *al-hadi* (the guide), *al-'alim* (the knowing), *al-sadiq* (the
truthful).

A tradition reported Yusuf ibn 'Atiyyah — who asked al-Kalbi for
the meaning of *kaf ha ya 'ain sad*, who in answer related a tradition
from Abu Salih, who heard it from 'Umm Hani, who quoted the
Apostle of God — as saying that the letters stood for *kafi* (all-sufficient), *hadi* (guide), *amin* (faithful), *'alim* (knowing) and *sadiq* (truthful).

A tradition by Ibn Abu Hatim, reported 'Ikrima as saying that the
letters mean that [God] says [in the Qur'an] that 'I am the Great One,
the Guide, the High, the Faithful, the Truthful'.

A tradition reported Muhammad ibn Ka'b as saying about *ta ha*[6]
that *ta* stands for *dhu 1 taul* (the Mighty One); *sin* for *quddus* (the Holy
One); and *mim* for *rahman* (the Merciful).

A tradition reported Sa'id ibn Jubair as saying about *ha mim* that *ha*
stands for *rahman* (the Merciful) and *mim* for *rahim* (the Compassionate).

A tradition reported Muhammed ibn Ka'b as saying about *ha mim
'ain sin qaf* that *ha* and *mim* stand for *rahman* (the Merciful), the *'ain*
for *'alim* (the All-Knowing), the *sin* for *quddus* (the Holy One) and the
qaf for *qahir* (the Conqueror).

A tradition reported Mujahid as saying that all the initial letters are
fragments of words.

A tradition reported Salim ibn 'Abdullah as saying that *alif lam mim,
ha mim* and *nun,* and the like, are abbreviations for the name of God.

A tradition reported al-Suddi as saying that the initial letters stand
for some of God's names, glory be to Him, scattered throughout the
Qur'an.

Al-Karmani said that the letter *qaf* was the initial letter of two of
God's attributes, *qadir* (the Powerful One) and *qahir* (the Conqueror).

Another view was that *nun* was the initial letter of two of God's attributes, may He be exalted, *nur* (light) and *nasir* (Conqueror).

These opinions amount to the view that the letters are abbreviations, and that each letter is derived from one of God's names, it being well known that part of a word in Arabic may stand adequately for the whole, as the poet has said:

Good attends on good and evil on evil.
I do not wish for evil unless you do.[7]

(The poet wrote *fa* in the first hemistich to stand for *fasharr;* and *ta* in the second for *tasha'.)*
And the poet said:

Will you not bridle your mounts, will you not ride?
And they all answered, 'Let us ride!'

(In this instance, the poet wrote *ta* for *tarkabun* and *fa* for *farkabu).*[8]

This interpretation was the one preferred by al-Zujja who said: The Arabs utter a single letter of a word to stand for the whole. And it is said that the initial letters are the greatest name of God, although we do not know how to compose it. This view was transmitted by Ibn 'Attiy-yah.

A tradition reported Ibn Jarir, citing an authentic chain of authorities deriving from Ibn Mas'ud, as saying that the letters are the greatest name of God.

A tradition by Ibn Abu Hatim, by way of al-Suddi, who claimed it reached him from Ibn Abbas, reported the latter as saying that the letters *alif lam mim* stand for one of the greatest names of God.

A tradition by Ibn Jarir and others, by way of Ali Ibn Abu Talha, reported Ibn Abbas as saying that *alif lam mim, ta sin mim* and *sad*, and the like, are an oath by which God swore, it being one of His names, and this may be taken as a third explanation (the other two being that the letters are fragments of words or that they are God's greatest name) that is that, generally speaking, the letters are God's names, and it is possible that this third explanation is of the same category as the first or the second. The first view [9] was held by Ibn Atiyyah and others. It is supported by a tradition from Ibn Maja in his *Tafsir*, by way of Nafi ibn Abu Nu'aim, the Reader, on the Authority of Fatimah, the daughter of 'Ali ibn Abu Talib, which reported that she heard 'Ali ibn Abu Talib say: 'O *kaf ha ya 'ain sad*, forgive me!'; also by a tradition by Ibn Abu Hatim which reported Rabi' ibn Anas as saying that *kaf ha ya 'ain sad* meant: 'O protector, whom none can defy!'

A tradition reported Ashhab as saying: ' I asked Malik ibn Anas, "Is it appropriate for someone to be named *ya sin?*" He replied, "I do not think it is appropriate, because God's word says, '*Ya sin* — By the wise Qur'an' [the opening of S. 36: 1], which means, 'Here is the name by which I am called'."

A tradition reported 'Abd al-Razzak, on the authority of Qatada, as saying that the letters are names of the Qur'an, such as *furqan* (deliverance) and *dhikr* (remembrance).

A tradition reported Ibn Abu Hatim as saying: 'Any such expression in the Qur'an is one of the names of the Qur'an itself.' According to another opinion transmitted by al-Mawardi and others on the authority of Zayd ibn Aslam, the letters are names of the Suras, a view which the author of the *Kashshaf* believed to be the majority opinion.

According to one opinion the letters are preludes to the Suras, like the particles *bal* (rather) and *la bal* (nay, rather) occurring as the first words of a poem.

A tradition transmitted by Ibn Jarir, by way of al-Thawri, from `Ibn Abu Najah, reported al-Mujahid as saying that the letters *alif lam mim, ha mim, alif lam mim sad,* and *sad,* and the like are God's preludes to the Qur'an.

A tradition transmitted by Abu al-Shaikh, by way of Ibn Jurayj, reported al-Mujahid as saying that *alif lam mim* and *alif lam mim ra* were God's preludes to the Qur'an. 'I said to him: "Did he not say that they were names?" He replied, "No." '

An opinion advanced by Abu Jad was that the letters had numerical values, indicating how long this [Islamic] nation would endure.

A tradition by Ibn Ishaq, by way of al-Kalbi, by way of Abu Salih, on the authority of Ibn Abbas, reported Jabir ibn 'Abdullah ibn Riyab as saying:

Abu Yasir ibn Akhtab, accompanied by some Jews, encountered the Prophet of God, God's blessing and peace be upon him, while he was reading the opening of the Sura entitled 'The Cow' [S. 2], which runs, '*Alif lam mim* — This is the Scripture whereof there is no doubt . . .' With the Jews, he then came to his brother Huyay and said: 'By God, do you know that I heard Muhammad read his revelation and say, "*Alif lam mim* — This is the Scripture . . ." ' He asked: 'You heard him yourself?' I replied, 'Yes, I did.'

So Huyay and the group went to the Prophet and said: 'Did you not mention *alif lam mim* on reading your revelation?' He said yes.

They said: 'God sent prophets before you, but we have not heard that He revealed to any one of them how long he would remain in power or the life-span of his community — except to you. For *alif* is one, *lam* is thirty, *mim* forty: a total of seventy-one years. Shall we then embrace the religion of a prophet whose rule and the life-span of whose community is seventy-one years!'

Then he said: 'O Muhammad! Have you any more [such letters]?' He answered, 'Yes, they are *alif lam mim sad.*' The man replied, 'These are more weighty and longer: *alif* is one; *lam* is thirty; *mim* forty and *sad* sixty. This makes a total of 131 years. Have you any more?' He said, 'Yes, *alif lam ra.*' He replied, 'These are still weightier and longer: *alif* is one; *lam* thirty; *ra* two hundred, making a total of 231 years. Have you any more?' He said, 'Yes, *alif lam mim ra.*' He replied, 'These are more weighty and longer still. They total 271.' Then he added, 'This is too abstruse for us, so that we cannot tell whether your rule will be long or short!' Then he said: 'Let us leave him.' Then Abu Yasir said to his brother and to those who were with him: 'How do you know? Perhaps all these numbers should be added up for Muhammad: 71 and twice 231 and 271, to total 704 years.' And they said, 'The matter is ambiguous.' And it is thought that because of them the verse in *The House of Imran* [S. 3: 7] was revealed: 'It is He who sent down upon thee the Book, wherein are verses clear that are the Essence of the Book, and others ambiguous.'

A tradition quoted Ibn Jarir in support of this view, also Ibn Mundhir, however, from another viewpoint, there is also a tradition quoting Ibn Jarir, but on doubtful authorities.

A tradition by Ibn Jarir and Ibn Abi Hatim reported Abu'l 'Aliya as saying concerning the letters *alif lam mim:*

There has been much discussion about these three letters out of the twenty-nine [of the alphabet]; every one of them is a key to one of the names of the Most High: every one is a blessing or a trial from God; every one is concerned with the span of men's lives and its termination. *Alif* is the key to the name of Allah; *lam* to the name *latif* (the Kind); *mim* to the name *majid* (the Glorious); and so the letter *alif* stands for *ala Allah* (God's gifts), and the *lam* stands for *lutf Allah* (God's kindness), and the *mim* stands for *majd Allah* (God's glory).

The *alif* also stands for one year, *lam* for thirty and *mim* for forty, according to al-Huwayyi, who said that some of the *imams* deduced from the passage *'alif lam mim* — The Greeks have been defeated [the opening of S. 30] that Jerusalem would be conquered by the Muslims in the year 583 — and it happened as was said. And al-Suhayli said: Perhaps the sum total of the letters at the beginning of the Suras, omitting repetitions, may point to the life-span of this community.

And Ibn Hajar said: This is baseless and cannot be relied upon, because it has been established from Ibn Abbas, may God be pleased with him, that Abu Jad's numerology must be dismissed — an indication that it must be classed as magic; and this is not far from the truth because it lacks roots in Islamic law. And the Qadi Abu Bakr ibn al-A'rabi said in his *Fawa 'id* that the science of the separate letters at the opening of the Suras was worthless. I have obtained a score of views and more on the subject, and I know of no one who accepts it as a science, or is any the wiser for it. What I would say is that if the Arabs had not recognised the letters as meaningful and in common use, they would have been the first to express their disapproval of the Prophet using them. But he read to them, *'Ha mim . . . fusilat'* [the opening of S. 41 runs: *'Ha mim* — This is revealed by the Compassionate, the Merciful: a Book of revelations well expounded *(fusilat)*, an Arabic Koran for men of understanding.'] and also *sad* [the opening letter of S. 38] and others, and they raised no objections, but rather applauded his eloquence and purity of diction, being ever on the watch for a slip or a lapse on his part, which demonstrates that [the meaning of the letters] was a well-known thing among them and could not be contested.

Another opinion was that the letters were signals, as if to call one to attention. According to Ibn Aliyyahm this view could not be reconciled with their being preludes, although the two ideas are on a par.

Abu 'Ubayda said: *Alif lam mim* are introductory. And al-Huwayyi said: The idea that they are signals is a good one, because the Qur'an is a precious word of great benefit, and it was therefore necessary that people should be alerted to hear it, and it is conceivable that God, knowing that the Prophet was sometimes occupied with things of this world, ordered Gabriel to recite *alif lam mim, alif lam ra, ha mim* when he descended, that the Prophet should hear the voice of Gabriel and come and listen to him. He said further: Admittedly, these letters are not ordinarily used for calling attention, as are such particles as *ala* ['is it not . . .'] and *ama* ['as for . . .'] , but these are expressions appropriate in common parlance. The Qur'an, however, is a Word not like ordinary speech: it is therefore appropriate that it should have signals not in ordinary use and that it should attack our hearing with greater seriousness.

Another view is that, when the Arabs heard the Qur'an, they recited it incorrectly, so God sent down this excellent system to astound them, so that their wonder might induce them to listen, not only to the letters but to what follows them, so that their hearts might be softened and their temper sweetened. Some consider the letters to be independent [from the text of the Qur'an] but this is patently wrong; however it may be applicable to some of them, because they have no meaning and they elucidate nothing.

Another view is that these letters are present to draw attention to the fact that the Qur'an is itself composed of letters, such as *alif ba ta tha* . . ., some of which occur disconnectedly and others in composition, to show the people in whose language the Qur'an was revealed and in letters with which they are familiar, that they may know and be convinced of their powerlessness to produce anything like it, seeing that it is revealed in letters which they know and from which they form their own speech.

Another view is that the intention behind the use of the letters — letters out of which speech is formed, fourteen letters in all, half of the alphabet — is to give half the number of every kind of letter occurring in the language. Thus, the gutturals are represented by *ha, 'ain* and *ha;* the palatals by *qaf* and *kaf;* the two labials by *mim;* the soft letters by *sin, ha, kaf, sad* and *ha;* the hard letters by *hamza, ta, qaf* and *kaf;* the voiced letters by *ta* and *sad;* the voiceless letters by *hamza, mim, lam, 'ain, ra, ta, qaf, ya* and *nun;* the open letters by *hamza, mim, ra, kaf, ha, 'ain, sin, ha, qaf, ya* and *nun;* the high-pitched letters by *qaf, sad* and *ta;* the muffled letters by *hamza, lam, mim, ra, kaf, ha, ya, 'ain, sin, ha* and *nun;* the convulsional letters by *qaf* and *ta.*

Moreover, the initial letters [in the Qur'an] come singly, or in twos, threes, fours or fives, but in no larger groupings, because the formation of words [in Arabic] never exceeds the use of five letters.

Another view is that the letters were intended by God as a sign to the People of the Book that a book was about to be revealed to Muhammad containing initial disjointed letters.

This is all I could gather concerning the subject of the letters, taken as a whole, but some of them may be differently explained.

One view is that *ta ha* and *ya sin* mean, 'O man!' or 'O Muhammad!' or 'O Human Being!'. This was explained in the section (of al-Suyuti's

Itqan) on Arabicised words of foreign origin. According to al-Karmani in his *Ghara'ib*, they stand for the Prophet's other names. This is corroborated by reading *ya sin* as *yasna* and by the name al-Yasin [in S.37: 130]. Another view is that *ta ha* stands for *ta al-ard*, 'subdue the earth', or *itma'inna*, 'rest assured'. In the first case, *ta* is an imperative and *ha* is a pronoun in the accusative, or it may be pausal *ha*, or a replacement for a *hamza*.

A tradition by Ibn Abu Hatim, by way of Sa'id ibn Jubayr, reported Ibn Abbas as saying that *ta ha* is as if one were to say: 'Do!' Another opinion cited by al-Karmani in his *Ghara'ib* is that *ta ha* means, 'O full moon!', on the argument that *ta* has a numerical value of nine and *ha* of five, making a total of fourteen (the day in the month when the moon is full).

Another view is that *ya sin* is an abbreviation for *ya sayyid al-mursalin*, 'O Chief of God's Messengers'; and that *sad* means 'God is true'. Or that it means, 'I Swear by *al-samad* [the Eternal], by *al-sani* [the Maker], by *al-sadiq* [the Truthful]'. Another view is that *sad* stands for *sadi,* meaning, 'Align your work, O Muhammad, on the Qur'an' — that is, compare it with the Qur'an.

A tradition reported al-Hussain as saying that [the meaning of *sad*] is, 'Ponder the events of the Qur'an', that is to say, look into it.

A tradition reported Sufian ibn Hussain as saying that Hasan's reading [of the opening verse of Sura 38] was *sadi wa'l qur'an,* which means *'arad al-qur'an,* that is to say 'compare the Qur'an'.

Another view is that *sad* was the name of a sea on which stood the throne of the Merciful; or that it was the name of the sea in which the dead will be raised to life. Another view is that it meant, 'Turn, O Muhammad, the hearts of God's servants'. All these views were held by al-Karmani.

And al-Karmani said that the letters *alif lam mim sad* [of S. 7] mean 'Did we not open up your heart for you' [the opening verse of S. 94]; and the letters *ha mim* stand for 'God's blessing and peace be upon him'; or that *ha mim* means 'All that exists'; and that the letters *ha mim 'ain sin qaf* refer to the Qaf mountain and that the letter *qaf* [of S. 50] refers to the mountain which encircles the earth. This is a tradition reported by 'Abd al-Razzaq on the authority of Mujahid.

Another view is that *qaf* means, 'I swear by the power of Muhammad's heart', or that it means, 'The matter is determined' [of S. 2: 210], pointing to the rest of the verse. Or that *qaf* means, 'Devote yourself, O Muhammad, to the propagation of the message and do that which you were commanded' — explanations which were transmitted by al-Karmani.

Another view is that the letter *nun* [of S. 68, 'The Pen'] stands for the fish, according to a tradition reported by al-Tabarini, on the authority of Ibn Abbas, from the Prophet, that the pen and the sea monster were the first of God's creation. God said [to the pen] : 'Write!' 'What shall I write?' [said the Pen] . He replied, 'Record all that exists until the Resurrection.' Hence the reading [of S. 68] *na wa'l qalam,* so that the *nun* stands for the fish and the *qaf* for the pen. Another view is that it refers to the Preserved Tablet. This tradition was reported by Ibn Jarir and Ibn Qurra, with a break in the chain of authorities going back to the Prophet.

A tradition reported al-Hasan and Qatada as saying that [the *nun*] stands for the inkpot. According to Ibn Qarsa in his *Gharib,* it stands for the ink. Or according to al-Karmani, on the authority of al-Jahiz, it stands for the pen.

Ibn 'Asakir, in his *Mubhamat,* said that it was one of the Prophet's names; and Ibn Jinni in his *Muhtasib* said that Ibn Abbas read the letters as *ha mim sin qaf,* omitting the *'ain,* saying that the *sin* meant that all factions would come into existence and that the *qaf* meant that every group would come into being.

According to Ibn Jinni, this reading indicates that the initial letters were marks to divide the Suras, for if they were divine names, no change in them would be permitted, for to make a change would mean they would be names no longer, because proper names must be given as they are, without change.

Commenting about *alif lam mim* – Do men think . . .? [the opening of S. 29] , al-Karmani said in his *Ghara'ib* that the question following the letters demonstrated that there was a break between the letters and what followed them in this and other Suras.

Notes

1. *ZDMG* vol. lxxv, 'Uber die Anordnung der Suren und uber die geheimnis-vollen Buchstaben in Qoran'.
2. *Der Islam,* vol. xiii, 'Ursprung und Bedeutung der Koranischen Siglen'.
3. *The Muslim World,* vol. xiv, July 1924.
4. Cf. Nöldeke-Schwally, *Geschichte,* p.36.
5. Arthur Jeffrey, *Materials for the History of the Text of the Qur'an,* Leiden, 1937.
6. The text is here in error. It should no doubt have read *ta sin mim* (ofS. 26 and 28).
7. The verse is by Wakid ibn 'Uqba in *Kitab al-Aghani,* V, 131.
8. For 'violent abbreviations' see Wright's *Grammar,* II, p. 381 d.
9. From the context it would seem to be the second.

4 THE NOMADIC BATTLE SONG OF JUDGES 5

A New Translation and Commentary

Scholars are agreed that Deborah's Ode of Judges 5 is one of the oldest passages in the Old Testament. It is also a work of great artistry. Perhaps because of its age, and because of the unfamiliar culture from which it stems, it contains Hebrew words and expressions which translators have found difficult to interpret, with the result that current translations differ markedly from one another. Alternative renderings abound in the margins and footnotes of the various editions testifying to the difficulties encountered by the translators, from the authors of the Authorised Version (AV) to those of the 1970 New English Bible (NEB). Where the text is obscure, and the ancient versions unhelpful, scholars have resorted to guesswork and suggestion, often pre-determined by their ideas of what this remarkable poem is about.[1]

What then *is* Deborah's poem about? The general view is that it is a psalm of thanksgiving addressed to Yahweh some three thousand years ago by the Hebrew prophetess and judge for the decisive victory which the Hebrews won over the Canaanite kings. Traditionally, a psalm is a hymn, a religious poem usually sung or declaimed as an act of worship. On this view, then, Deborah's Ode is a hymn of praise.

I hope to demonstrate below that this view of the poem is untenable. Accordingly, a new interpretation is advanced together with a new translation which will allow the work to be seen in a new light. My argument is that the Ode is not a hymn of thanksgiving but a battle song; not a religious work but an essentially secular one. Finally, I want to show that the *genre* to which it belongs is that of nomadic war poetry, identical with battle songs found in ancient Arabian literature.

A generation ago, C.F. Burney, in his definitive study of the Book of Judges (first published in 1918), pointed out that a number of words used in the Song of Deborah could only be explained by recourse to a cognate language such as Arabic. This was not to say that Arabic influenced the language of the Song; rather that, as Hebrew and Arabic were of common stock, and as our knowledge of Arabic vocabulary was much more extensive than our knowledge of Hebrew — Hebrew literature being extremely limited — it was legitimate to turn to Arabic to help us explain some otherwise obscure Hebrew words which were

most probably in common use when the Song was composed.[2] I would
go further: not only is Arabic invaluable in elucidating etymological
obscurities in the Hebrew text; it is also the key to an ancient nomadic
culture which enables us to understand the pervading tribal spirit of
Deborah's Song.

Deborah's Ode: A New Translation

1. That day Deborah and [or, in the company of] Barak,
    Abinoam's son, sang this song.

2. When locks hung wild in Israel,
    When the people nobly offered their services,
    Praise the Lord!

3. Hear, O Kings; listen, you princes.
    I will sing to Yahweh, I will praise on a reed pipe
    The God of Israel.

4. When you set out from Seir,
    When you stepped forth from the field of Edom,
    Earth trembled, heavens flowed,
    Dense clouds poured water.

5. Mountains dissolved because of Yahweh,
    Even Sinai in face of Yahweh, the God of Israel.

6. In the days of Shamgar, Anath's son,
    In the days of Jael, journeying by caravan halted,
    Travellers on foot took to side roads.

7. Unprotected hamlets were abandoned in Israel,
    Until I, Deborah, arose,
    Rose up to be a mother in Israel.

8. God chose to do new things.
    There was fighting at the fronts.
    Shield and spear were hardly seen
    Among the forty thousand fielded by Israel.

9. My heart goes out to the commanders of Israel,
    To the noble people who volunteered.
    Praise the Lord!

10. Those who travel on tawny she-asses,
    Those who are settled,
    Those who walk the roads on foot,

Talk about it.

11. Louder than the splashing at the well-head
Where the buckets are lowered and raised,
There they recite the mighty deeds of Yahweh,
His mighty generosity in Israel.
Then down to the fronts went Yahweh's people.

12. Rouse, O rouse yourself, Deborah,
Rouse yourself, rouse yourself, and sing.
Up Barak! Take prisoners in plenty,
Abinoam's son.

13. A mail-clad warrior rushed down to the skin-clad men,
The people of the Lord joined me among the heroes.

14. From Ephraim captains [went down into] the valley,
'We are behind you with your clansmen, Benjamin.'
From Machir came the commanders,
From Zebulun those who wield the recruiters' truncheons.

15. The chieftains of Issacher are with Deborah,
Issacher, and also Barak
Sent down into the valley with his foot soldiers.
Reuben, split into factions, great is their baseness of heart.

16. Why do you tarry between the animal paddocks
To hear the shrill halloos among the flocks?
Reuben, split into factions, great is their baseness of heart.

17. Gilead dwells across the Jordan;
And Dan, why does he tarry with the ships?
Asher settled on the coast,
Making his home by the inlets.

18. Zebulun is a clan which holds its life in contempt to the point of
death,
As does Naphtali on the heights of the battlefield.

19. Kings came, they fought;
Then fought the kings of Canaan
At Taanach by the waters of Megiddo;
They were not prompted by gain.

20. The heavens joined the conflict,
The stars in their courses battled with Sisera.

21. The torrent of wadi Kishon swept him away,

The wadi of the front-line heroes,
The Kishon wadi.
On to glory, my soul!

22.   Then drummed the hooves of horses,
His great beasts prancing, prancing.

23.   Curse Meroz, curse it, said the angel of the Lord,
Accursed be its inhabitants,
Because they failed to come to aid the Lord,
To aid Yahweh and the heroes.

24.   Blessed among women be Jael,
The spouse of Heber the Kenite;
Blessed among women in the tent.

25.   Water he asked for, milk she gave,
In a lordly bowl she brought him curds,

26.   Her hand reached for the tent-peg,
Her right hand for the workmen's mallet.
She hammered Sisera, she destroyed his head;
She stabbed and pierced his temple.

27.   He tumbled to his knees, he fell at her feet, he lay still.
At her feet, he sank to his knees and fell.
Where he tumbled, there he fell dead.

28.   Looking out from the window, crying out
At the peep-hole, is the mother of Sisera:
'Why is his chariot so late in coming?
Why so long delayed is the clatter of his chariots?'

29.   Her wise, high-born ladies answer her.
She makes her own reply:

30.   'Are they not finding and dividing loot,
A wench or two for every man,
Booty of dyed stuff for Sisera,
Booty of coloured embroidery,
Coloured embroidered fabrics,
Two lengths each for the necks of the spoilers?'

31.   So perish all your enemies, Yahweh.
And may those who love him be as the midday sun.

Commentary

V.1.   The introductory verse, evidently the work of an editor, attributes the Song to both Deborah and Barak. But, as may be seen from Ju.4: 6, Barak was the fighting man upon whom she had called, in Yahweh's name, to raise a force which he then led into battle. No doubt the text links his name with hers in the opening verses because of his role in the field. As is evident from *v*.12, he did the fighting and she the singing. Clearly, Deborah, the prophetess, was the sole author of the poem.

V.2   In this second introductory verse the tone of the whole poem is set succinctly in two short phrases. The first line describes tribesmen in battle, their hair hanging loose and dishevelled. This is the sense of the Hebrew expression *bi-pro'a pra'oth,* as found also, for example, in Leviticus 10: 6, 13: 45 and 21: 10, where the same root *p-r-'* is used to describe 'loose, wild and unbraided hair'. A similar account of tribal fighters is found in Arabian poetry, as for example in Abu Tammam's *Hamsa,* 'Riders dishevelled with locks caked in dust'.[3]

These wild fighters are described in the second line of the verse as nobly volunteering their lives in the cause, a virtue also extolled in *v*.9.

Vv.3-5 The prelude   What is the significance of these opening verses? Are they related to the rest of the poem or do they stand apart? C.F. Burney connects the thunderstorm described in *vv*.4 and 5 with the discomfiture of Deborah's enemies in the body of the poem.[4] A similar link is forged by G.A. Cook who asserts that *vv*.4 and 5 'describe the aweful coming of Jehovah to help his people in the battle' and that the Godhead was 'in the storm which brough disaster upon Sisera's army'.[5] A more recent commentator, James D. Martin, writes that the 'first part of the poem . . . looks as if it belongs within a context of worship . . . Some of the language . . . is very like the kind of language used in the Psalms'.[6]

Such analyses, connecting the opening verses to the later narrative, or seeing them as elements in a liturgy, fail to recognise the conventional literary nature of *vv*.3-5. They form a prelude in praise of Yahweh, a literary device in common use by Hebrew poets. Standing at the head of a poem, such preludes bear no relation at all to the subject matter dealt with in the poem. This may be seen from other biblical preludes, in all of which the mountains flow and the earth quakes in God's presence. Examples may be found in Ps.68: 8 and 97: 4f; in Mic.1: 3f; in Hab.3: 3-7 and in 2 Sam.22: 8-16 (although in this last case the prelude has been slightly displaced, perhaps by an editor, and begins at *v*.8).

There is an echo in many of these preludes of the theophany on Sinai on the occasion of the giving of the Law, when 'there were thunders and lightnings, and a thick cloud upon the mount . . . and the whole mount quaked greatly' (Ex.19: 16, 18). Clearly the account of these events had a profound impact on the mind of the Hebrew poet, leaving its stamp on the style and content of traditional preludes. It is significant that Sinai is mentioned in three of them, in Deut. 33, Ps. 68 and in Ju. 5: 5.

External evidence from the cognate Arabic supports the view that *vv*. 3-5 are a conventional prelude. Large numbers of Arabian odes open with a prelude, usually of an erotic nature, in which the poet, on visiting a deserted encampment, evokes nostalgic memories of his departed beloved. But instead of celebrating the joys of physical love, the preludes of the biblical Hebrew songs sing of God's power and glory. They are theophanies, that is to say they speak of the manifestation of God's power in nature. Such awesome descriptions of the appearance of God were the objects of the Hebrew poet's worship replacing the erotic preludes of the pagan nomad.[7]

Vv. 6-11   This passage sets the scene for the battle, mentioning the general state of insecurity and the excited climate of opinion — a mixture of apprehension and pride — as Yahweh's people head for the front.

V. 7   Commentators have wrestled to make sense of this verse, and, in particular, with the word *prazon*, which also occurs in *v*. 11. G. Gerleman says the word is wholly unknown;[8] and because of it, G.F. Moore writes off *v*. 11 as an 'unintelligible and indubitably corrupt text'. He says further that 'the text of these verses [9 to 11] has suffered so badly that there is no reasonable hope that any art or skill by the critic will ever be able to restore it'.[9]

This puzzlement over the meaning of *prazon*, or rather *prazoth* as found in four Massoretic manuscripts, is reflected in the various versions of *v*. 7. The Authorised Version rendering is: 'The inhabitants of the villages ceased . . . ' The Jerusalem Bible says: 'Dead, dead were Israel's villages.' The New English Bible writes: 'Champions there were none, none left in Israel.' This appears to be an occasion where the oldest translation is closest to the original meaning. As C.F. Burney has pointed out, *prazoth* are 'unwalled, unprotected hamlets' whose inhabitants must have taken refuge in caves or hills when war came their way — a perilous state of affairs which persisted 'Until I, Deborah, arose . . . '.

V. 8   C.F. Burney holds that this verse is the most difficult to interpret — 'perhaps the greatest crux in the poem'.[10] The AV and the NEB
are obviously wrong in rendering the opening line of the verse as 'They
chose new gods'. Such an act of apostasy is a *non sequitur* in the context and a totally unjustified interpretation. How can a passage dealing
with the bravery and daring of the poorly-armed Israelites confronting
the Canaanite war-machine be introduced by the mention of new gods
(or indeed demons, as the NEB further ventures)? Burney mentions
in parentheses, without further comment, the suggestion that the first
hemistich could be rendered as 'God chooses new things'[11] — which
makes excellent sense, and is supported by the Peshitta.[12] It may also
be remarked that the Hebrew *hadashi,* 'new things', is the equivalent
of the Arabic *hawadith*, 'events' or 'new developments'. The word is
found, for example, in a passage of Arabian war poetry:

> Lions are Mazin's people, eminent riders are they,
>   Spear thrust for spear thrust they mete out;
> Meet them and their patience you will know,
>   When troubles come and *events* befall.[13]

In Deborah's poem, the 'new things' spoken of are the battles
raging at the frontiers which are referred to in the second hemistich
— a line which has also posed considerable problems to the translators.
Both the Authorised and the Revised versions run: 'then was war in
the gates,' a rendering from which the NEB radically departs with its
'they consorted with demons' (or satyrs, as a footnote adds). Stranger
still, the Jerusalem Bible translates the two hemistichs as: 'Those that
should stand for God were dumb.'

The problem centres around the Hebrew word *sha'n*, which the AV
translates as 'gates' and the NEB as 'demons'. Indeed, much scholarly
ingenuity has been expended on interpreting this word.[14] But recourse
to the cognate Arabic shows that the Hebrew word is the equivalent of
the Arabic *thaghr*, meaning a 'frontier'. The context supports this
translation as it does on many other occasions where the word is
found. For example, Ps. 127: 3-5 which, in the Jerusalem Bible version,
reads:

> Sons are a bounty from Yahweh,
> he rewards with descendants:
> Like the arrows in a Hero's hand
> are the sons you father when young.

> Happy the man who has filled his quiver
> with arrows of this sort;
> in dispute with his enemies at the gate,
> he will not be worsted.

Sha'r does commonly mean a 'gate', but it has a second meaning which Arabic helps us grasp, namely a 'breach in a wall', a 'frontier' — the spot where one defends oneself against external attack.

V. 9   The noun to which I would draw attention here is *nadib*, 'noble', equivalent to the Arabic *karim*, which means both 'noble' and 'generous'. The ascription of nobility carries no connotation of noble birth, but is rather a conventional complimentary form of address. To this day, an Arab, addressing an audience, would say: 'O noble assembly . . .' This style of address is found in Num. 21: 18 where the original text reads 'noble people'. In Ju. 5: 9, however, as in *v*.2, the people are not only called 'noble' but are also rightly praised for volunteering for battle.

V. 10   The puzzle in this verse concerns not those who ride on asses, nor those who walk on foot, but the third group who, in my rendering, are 'settled'. The AV translates the line as 'Ye that sit in judgement' and the NEB as 'you that sit on saddle cloths'. Both these seem far-fetched. The Hebrew word is *middin* which I connect with the Arabic root *madana*, 'to settle in a place', 'to become sedentary'. What the verse seems to say is that news of the victory was discussed everywhere, by people on the move, roaming or migrating, as well as by the sedentary population. The reader will note a similarity between *vv*. 6 and 7 on the one hand and *v*.10 on the other. Both passages refer to three groups of people: mounted travellers, pedestrians, and the settled part of the population.

V. 11   Translators have found this verse particularly difficult. The Authorised Version is: 'They that are delivered from the noise of archers in the places of drawing water . . .', while the NEB proposes: 'Hark, the sound of the players striking up in the places where the women draw water!' Clearly, neither is wholly satisfactory. Much of the difficulty relates to the word *mehasesim* which scholars have wrestled with, translating it variously as 'archers' (RV), 'musicians' (RSV), 'maidens laughing' (C.F. Burney), 'players' (NEB), 'rejoicing people' (Jerusalem Bible).

A possible solution to the puzzle is provided by the Arabic *khadda*, 'to stir', or 'jolt', together with *khadkad*, meaning the 'sound of moving, splashing water'. The Arabic word is identical to the Hebrew root in question (the Hebrew letter *sadi* being the equivalent of the Arabic *dad*). This justifies my translation: 'Louder than the splashing at the well-head.' The verse carries forward and develops the sense of *v*.10, relating how the battle, and the victory which crowned it, were spoken of everywhere, drowning the bustle at the water-point, the obvious centre for gossip and exchange of news.

Another expression in the verse which needs explanation is *sidqoth*, from *s'daqah*, customarily rendered as 'righteousness'. In this context, where I translate it as 'mighty deeds', reference may be made to the cognate Arabic noun *sadq*, which means the 'fine quality of a blade', and hence a man wielding such a blade and also the booty such a blade could win and hold. With the coming of Yahwistic morality, when wars were no longer waged only for loot, a 'warrior' became a 'righteous man'. *S'daqah* took on an ethical connotation: 'mighty deeds' became 'righteous acts'.[15]

In the following hemistich, the phrase *sidkoth pirzono*, which I translate as 'his mighty generosity', has also been a cause of difficulty. The AV renders it as 'the righteous acts towards the inhabitants of his villages', while the NEB prefers 'his triumphs as the champions of Israel'. Neither can be judged satisfactory. In my view *pirzon* is a corruption of *pizron*, with the two radicals '*r*' and '*z*' transposed. One can imagine a scribe making just such a mistake, seeing that he had written *prazon* a moment earlier in *v*.7. In any event there is nothing arbitrary in transposing two radicals and there are several biblical instances of such transposition. *Kebhes* and *kesebh* are both used in the Bible to mean a 'sheep', just as *simlah* and *salmah* are used to mean a 'cloak' or 'robe'. Such interchange of positions between sounds or letters in a word is known as metathesis, a phenomenon not uncommon in Arabic poetry. If this is accepted, it will be seen that *pizron* is derived from the verb *pizzer* of Ps. 112: 9, 'to give generously', hence its meaning of 'generosity' in this context.

V. 12   James D. Martin, in his commentary on the Book of Judges, casts doubt on the NEB rendering: 'Rouse, rouse yourself, Deborah, Rouse yourself, lead out the host.'[16] There is indeed no justification for this flagrant departure in the second hemistich from the original text which in this instance poses no problems. The AV version: 'Awake, Deborah ... utter a song' is correct. Both the prose version of the battle in Judges 4 and Deborah's own poem agree on the different role played by the prophetess and by Barak, her field commander: she initiated the recourse to arms and, at the end of the day, sang the victory song, but it was he who led the host into battle.

V. 13   This verse is generally accepted as obscure, as may be judged from the various renderings. The Authorised version reads:

> Then he made him that remaineth have dominion over the nobles among the people: the Lord made me have dominion over the mighty.

This may be contrasted with the New English Bible version:

> Then down marched the column and its chieftains,
> the people of the Lord marched down like warriors.

In its turn, the Jerusalem Bible says:

> Then Israel marched down to the gates;
> Yahweh's people, like heroes, marched down to fight for him.

There is much that is unsatisfactory with all three versions. Let us first examine the narrative context in which the verse occurs. Barak, the commander, has just been urged in the preceding passage to enter the fray: we may expect this to be followed by a description of how he sets about it. But the three renderings above do not carry the story forward, except perhaps for the NEB version which does convey the sense of troops on the move. However, it, too, misses the real meaning of the two key words used in the hemistich, *sarid* and *addirim*.

I would propose the following rendering:

> A mail-clad warrior rushed down to the skin-clad men;
> The people of the Lord joined me among the heroes.

This translation is based essentially on an interpretation of *sarid* as 'mail-clad warrior' and *addirim* as 'skin-clad men'.

Let us first examine *sarid*. I would relate it to the Arabic verb *sarada*, 'to weave a coat of mail', and also to the Hebrew *bigdai ha-s' rad* of Exodus 31: 10 and 35: 19, where it refers to the high-priestly garments which were overlaid and interwoven with precious metal, as described in Exodus 39: 3: 'And they did beat the gold into thin plates, and cut it into wires, to work it in the blue and in the purple . . .' I would also relate it to the Aramaic *s'rada*, meaning 'latticed', that is to say wood or metal crossed and fastened together.[17] What the verse describes is Barak, in full armour, joining his somewhat less well-equipped troops in the field. One may suppose that his gear resembled Saul's armour as described in 1 Sam. 17: 38.

As for *addirim*, I would connect it with the hair-cloak *addereth se'ar* (Gen. 25: 25) in which Essau appeared to be covered at birth, such was the growth of hair on him. Yahweh's warriors were evidently wearing animal skins with the hair on the outside. *Addirim* are those who wore *addereth*, hence 'skin-clad'.

V. 14 As we learn from Judges 4: 6, Zebulun and Naphtali provided the bulk of the fighting force — ten thousand men. This may explain the flattering reference to Zebulun's recruiting officers.

V. 15 There are two main difficulties in this verse of which the first concerns the reference to Barak. In the Authorised version, Barak is sent 'upon foot' into the valley. The NEB evades the issue by omitting all reference to feet (*b'raglaw*, in the original). C.F. Burney renders the Hebrew phrase as 'at his heel'[18] which is evidently mistaken. The preposition *b'* means 'with', while *raglaw*, from the singular *ragli*, as in 2 Sam. 8: 4, means 'foot-soldiers'. It is obvious, then, that Barak was sent with his infantry to do battle in the valley. Hence, *vv.* 12, 13 and 15 sum up the part played by Barak in the fighting.

A real puzzle is posed by the reference to Reuben in both *vv.* 15 and 16, which the authorised version renders first as 'there were great thoughts of heart' and then as 'there were great searchings of heart'. The NEB settles for 'great were their heart-searchings' in *v.* 15, but omits it altogether in *v.*16. I would hazard the proposal that the Hebrew *hikrai* in this passage is derived from the same root as the Arabic *hakira* 'to be mean and despicable', hence my translation of *g'dolim hikrai lebh* as 'great is their baseness of heart'. That Reuben's character was already reprehensible may be learned from Gen. 49: 4.

Vv. 16, 17 These verses portray and condemn the clans that stayed away from the battle, beginning with the Reubenites. As we know from Numbers 32, the Reubenites were owners of large flocks of sheep and herds of cattle — so much so that when they found good grazing country in Jazer and Gilead east of the Jordan, they refused to cross

the river with the rest of the Israelites. 'We will build folds for our
sheep here and towns for our dependents,' they said (Num. 32: 16).
Furthermore, in Jos. 22: 9, Gilead is described as 'the land which
belonged to them' (together with the Gadites and one half of the tribe
of Manasseh). With this background in mind, Deborah's reference to
the Reubenites becomes clear: she contemptuously depicts them as
refusing to budge from their animal pens in Gilead across the Jordan.

V. 18   The word in this verse which has mainly puzzled translators
is *heref*, which the NEB renders as 'risked', in the line: 'The people of
Zebulun risked their very lives.' This fairly conveys the meaning of the
original, although it omits the finer shades. In many biblical passages,
heref means 'to defy', as in 1 Sam. 17: 26 where David says: 'Who is
this uncircumcised Philistine, that he should *defy* the armies of the
living God?' It is also used to mean 'to defy or insult God, or profane
his name', as in Isaiah 65: 7 where the Israelites 'blasphemed' God by
burning incense to idols on hill tops. In effect, they held God in contempt, and it is this sense of the word which is found in Judges 5: 18
where the Zebulun tribesmen are said 'to hold their life in contempt'.
The same sentiment is expressed in Arabian poetry where tribal warriors
prided themselves on their readiness to die in battle: 'We are a people
who do not consider being slain a blot ... No Lord of ours ever dies
in his bed ... our lifeblood, along the blade's sharp edge, courses
away; we refuse to die in any other way.'[19]
   Naphtali fought with reckless courage 'on the heights of the battlefield'. High ground in tribal encounters was tactically the best terrain
to fight from, or the place to run to in defeat. The mountain tops or
ridges were the nomad's most secure haven. That the dead in David's
lament (2 Sam. 1: 19) were lying on the heights meant that the disaster
was complete: Israel had been defeated in a place of traditional safety
and strength. Another reference to the 'heights' (Hebrew, *bamoth*)
occurs in Deut. 33: 29 which, literally rendered, runs: 'Your enemies
will deny their true feelings [of hostility] and you will trample on
their high places.' This simply means that you will defeat them and
occupy their strongholds, a sense the NEB misses in its translation:
'Your enemies come cringing to you, and you shall trample their bodies
under foot.'

V. 21   The Hebrew *nahal*, like the more familiar Arabic *wadi*, means
a ravine or valley which, in the rainy season, turns with lightning
suddenness into a torrent. The rush of water can strike like a whip

(Hebrew, *shot*) as in Isaiah 28: 18: 'When the destructive whip goes by it will crush you' (Jerusalem Bible). In order to convey the ambiguity of a term which can mean both 'valley' and 'flood', depending on the season, I have rendered *nahal kishon* as 'the torrent of wadi Kishon'. The elements evidently came to the aid of the Israelites: a rainstorm flooded the wadi, grounding Sisera's iron chariots and scattering his panic-stricken men, allowing them to be cut down by Barak's troops (Ju. 4: 13-16 and Ju. 5: 21).

In the second hemistich, the Kishon is described as *nahal k'dumim,* an expression which has posed considerable problems to generations of scholars and commentators. It has been variously rendered as the 'ancient river' (AV); the 'sacred torrent' (Jerusalem Bible); 'the torrent barred his flight' (NEB, in a daring departure from the text); and the 'onrushing torrent' (Meier, Cooke, Grimme and Driver). However, reviewing the literature on the poem, C.F. Burney mentions that G.F. Moore (in his International Critical Commentary on Judges) noted that the Hebrew *k'dumim* was identical with the Arabic *kadum*, meaning 'a man who is first in attacking a foe' — and hence 'brave' or 'courageous'. Thus the Hebrew phrase would mean 'the torrent of heroes'.[20] Burney refers to Moore's finding, but fails to adopt it, preferring to render the Hebrew phrase *nahal k'dumim* as: 'It faced them, the torrent Kishon.'

In my view, Moore was most certainly on the right track in seeking elucidation from the cognate Arabic. I would therefore suggest that the right translation is: 'The wadi of the front-line heroes'; this best conveys Deborah's meaning that it was in the wadi Kishon, swollen by rain, that Barak's front-line troops routed the Canaanites. The Arabic *kadama* means 'to advance boldly against an enemy'. The usefulness of Arabic seems indisputable, not just in this particular case but throughout the poem.

The conclusion of the strophe, *tidreki nafsi 'oz*, has again bewildered the commentators, with the AV rendering it as: 'O my soul, thou has trodden down strength.' The NEB version, 'March on in might, my soul!' is an improvement, although still not wholly satisfactory. The Hebrew noun *'oz* occurs no fewer than 164 times in the Old Testament, and has traditionally been rendered as 'strength' or 'might' as in Exodus 15: 2 — 'The Lord is my strength [*'oz*] and song' (AV and RSV). (The NEB unaccountably renders the verse as: 'The Lord is my refuge and my defence.' In my view *'oz* is a key term, not only in a nomadic vocabulary, but also in nomadic consciousness, and I am convinced that it has other and perhaps more important connotations than

'strength'. These further meanings may be elucidated by reference to
the cognate Arabic *'izz*, which means 'honour', 'glory'. 'self-esteem',
even 'haughtiness'. Its opposite is not 'weakness', but 'servility' and
'docility'. For the nomad in Arabian society *'izz* was dearer than life
itself: he preferred death to humiliation.[21] With this in mind, we can
better render the final line of Judges 5: 21 as: 'On to glory, my soul!'

As James D. Martin has remarked, many scholars have emended
the text in an attempt to make sense of it,[22] comparing it with Psalm
103: 1, 2 — 'Bless the Lord, my soul' — and producing the rendering
'Bless, O my soul, the might of the Lord'.[23] But such tampering with
the original text is unproductive and unnecessary seeing that 'On to
glory, my soul!' makes good sense. (It may be worth mentioning that
the Hebrew *tidreki* is a jussive standing for an imperative, but this is
by no means exceptional. For example, a similar use of the jussive is
found several times in Ps. 51: 8, 9 and 10).

Vv. 23 and 24   These are chiefly remarkable for their implacable
spirit: Meroz is cursed repeatedly for staying away from the battle,
while Jael is extravagantly praised for slaying Sisera, even though the
deed was done in a flagrant breach of nomadic hospitality. The whole
passage savours of the desert and is similar in tone to the imprecatory
Psalms where enemies are cursed and their destruction gloated over.

V. 25   The Hebrew expression *sefel addirim* has been variously
rendered as a 'lordly dish' (AV); a 'lordly bowl' (RSV); and a 'bowl fit
for a chieftain' (NEB). In a nomadic society, the size of one's cooking
and serving dishes was an index of one's generosity, and hence a status
symbol. *Sefel addirim* means no more than a 'large dish'. As we saw it
in the commentary to *v*. 13 above, *addirim* in that context meant
'skin clad', hence a 'warrior' or 'chieftain'. In the desert, where a
single wrap was the rule, clothes made the man. To wear ankle-length
raw-hide apparel denoted a man of substance and might.

V. 26   The Hebrew expression *halmuth 'amelim*, which I have rendered
as 'workmen's mallet', has been a cause of difficulty as some translators,
including the authors of the NEB, have taken *'amelim* to mean 'weary'.
C.F. Burney, in an exhaustive examination of the term, rightly points
out that the cognate languages prove that the root can be used in the
general sense of 'work'.[24] The Arabic *amila* means 'to work' and *'amil*
is a 'workman'. It is curious that the NEB disregarded Burney's researches.

V. 27   From the prose version in Judges 4:21, it would appear that Jael attacked Sisera when he lay asleep, so the poetic account in which he tumbles to his knees and falls dead would seem to be a discrepancy. This verse may perhaps best be seen as a formal account of the killing of an enemy in a nomadic engagement. The climax of such a confrontation was to bring the opponent to his knees and kill him. The Hebrew *kara'* in the verse means literally 'to go down on one's knees'.[25] The thrice-repeated account of the action in which Sisera fell to his death is characteristic of the poem's style, in which repetition for dramatic effect is frequently used.

Vv. 28-30   This is a satirical passage, mocking the enemy and gloating over his downfall, in a manner and spirit characteristic of desert vengefulness. It may be compared with Isaiah's savage satire on the tyrannical King of Babylon (Isa. 14). The effective repitition and combination of the terms meaning 'dyed stuff' and 'embroidery' provide another example of the poem's style referred to in the preceeding comment.

V. 31   Commentators are divided as to whether this final verse, which stands on its own, is part of the original poem or a later addition. Whatever the verdict, it brings to a conclusion a nomadic war-song only somewhat tempered by a knowledge of Yahweh.

Notes

1. For an able review of the literature see James D. Martin, *The Book of Judges* (The Cambridge Bible Commentary, 1975), p. 62ff.
2. C.F. Burney, *The Book of Judges*, London, 3rd edn, 1930, p. 171.
3. Abu Tammam, *Hamasa* (Cairo), I, p. 259. See also M.S. Seale, *The Desert Bible*, pp. 27-8.
4. C.F. Burney, *The Book of Judges*, p. 112.
5. G.A. Cook, *Judges* (Cambridge Bible), p. 55.
6. James D. Martin, *The Book of Judges*, p. 67.
7. For a more detailed account of Arabian and Hebrew preludes see M.S. Seale, *The Desert Bible*, pp. 64-9.
8. G. Gerleman, 'The Song of Deborah in the Light of Stylistics', *Vet. Test.* (1951), pp. 168ff.
9. G.F. Moore, *Judges*, International Critical Commentary, pp. 144, 146.
10. C.F. Burney, *The Book of Judges*, p. 117.
11. C.F. Burney, *The Book of Judges*, p. 117.
12. C.F. Burney, *The Book of Judges*, p. 118.
13. *Al-Hamasa*, I, 124.
14. C.F. Burney, *The Book of Judges*, pp. 117-19.
15. See M.S. Seale, *The Desert Bible*, p. 204.
16. James D. Martin, *The Book of Judges*, p. 70.

18. C.F. Burney, *The Book of Judges*, p. 138.
19. *Al-Hamasa*, I, 111.
20. C.F. Burney, *The Book of Judges*, pp. 147-8.
21. See M.S. Seale, *The Desert Bible*, pp. 200-2, for a further elucidation of the term.
22. James D. Martin, *The Book of Judges*, p. 74.
23. C.F. Burney, *The Book of Judges*, p. 149.
24. C.F. Burney, *The Book of Judges*, pp. 153-4.
25. See M.S. Seale, *The Desert Bible*, p. 197, for a further elucidation of this term.

5 JOHN OF DAMASCUS: A DIALOGUE BETWEEN A SARACEN AND A CHRISTIAN

Introduction

Dialogue between religions has become a fashionable concern, particularly in the new climate of tolerance now prevalent between members of different faiths. The accent in such present-day exchanges is less to score points and reduce one's opponent to silence, than to draw him out in charity and share with him what one has found helpful and enlightening in one's own religion. The time is past when disputants hurled rival texts at each other, often drawn from each other's sacred books, in an attempt to strengthen their own case.

The famous dialogue of John of Damascus with the Saracen is not, it need hardly be said, in this modern tradition. It is a manual of dialectics, a text-book exercise in punishing argument. John's objective was to provide a model for eighth-century Christians to equip them intellectually in their dealings with the conquering Muslims. The pattern of questions and answers, of traps and theological pitfalls, of stratagems and rhetorical devices, was intended to instruct the Christian in the mind and tactics of his Muslim opponent. The ideal was so to out-manoeuvre and outwit the enemy as to impale him on the horns of a dilemma. Victory consisted in compelling the antagonist to admit that he had 'nothing more to say'.

It is evident that John's Dialogue is a literary *genre*, a formal display of intellectual thrust and counter-thrust, rather than actual dialogue which took place with a real Saracen. Indeed, the Saracen remains nameless; his role may be compared to that of a sparring partner. But if the framework of the dialogue is formal, its content is not. The questions raised and the answers they inspire are very real and of abiding interest: it is curious to note that they have their exact parallels in the Muslim world today. Wherever Christian meets Muslim these matters are debated in much the same terms. This is what gives John's Dialogue its great actuality.

In eighth-century Damascus, John was known as Mansur ibn Sarjun, a government official as was his father before him in the service of the Umayyads. To us today he is Saint John of Damascus, theologian, hymnographer and Father of the Church. A Greek biographer of John tells the story that, accused of a treasonable correspondence with

Byzantium, he had an arm struck off by the Muslim rulers of Damascus. (Legend has it that the Virgin restored the severed limb.) In any event, something dreadful appears to have happened to him during his career as a government servant. The Dialogue carries a hint of it, conveyed in the most elliptical terms. John declares that God, wishing him to repent, 'dealt with him as he did with the Jews'. Is this an oblique reference to his punishment? The clear suggestion is that he was humbled. I should like to see in the incident a clue to his saintliness.

There are one or two questions raised in the Dialogue which deserve a word of explanation. The first concerns the problem of free will which occupies a central place in Muslim theology. The Saracen, it will be noted, asks: 'Have you then free will, and can you do what you wish?' The tone is one of amazement. This reflects the fact that all orthodox Muslim theologians, basing themselves on the *Hadith*, were predestinarians, denying man freedom of the will. This was the common position, and not only that of the extremist *Jabriyya* who, as their name indicates, believed that man acts under 'compulsion'. A characteristic statement of this position may be found in the teaching of Jahm ibn Safwan, executed in 746, who held that man was a mere puppet, dependent on God even for the mechanism of movement. Even theologians who did not hold this extreme *Jabriyya* doctrine still denied man any *qadar* or free will. Hence, in the Dialogue, John's counter-argument is that only by granting man a measure of free will can he be held responsible for his misdeeds.

A second point very much in dispute between Christians and Muslims concerns the divinity of Christ. The Saracen raises the matter in the Dialogue by posing the question: 'Who was Christ?' To win him over to the Christian view of Jesus, John deploys what he believes is his powerful argument. He gets the Saracen to admit that the Qur'an calls Christ a 'Spirit from God' (S. 4: 169) and, in another passage, the 'Word of truth' (S. 19: 35). The next stage in John's argument is to point out that, as God could never have been without spirit or word, his 'Spirit' and 'Word' must therefore be eternal, and because eternal, therefore divine. (Needless to say, the Qur'an in fact denies the divinity of Christ: to the Muslim, the uncreated Word is not a person but a Book.)

Finally, one further question often divides Christians and Muslims — that of Christ's death, the 'scandal' of the crucifixion. John attempts to explain how God could have allowed it to take place, in the face of the Saracen's view, supported by the Qur'an, that it never happened. The cross was possible, John says, not because God willed it, but because of his 'tolerance, endurance and patience'.

The Dialogue

[Translated from the Greek text in J.P. Migne, *Patrologica Græca*, vol. 96, pp. 1335-47, Paris, 1864.]

If you are asked by the Saracen, What do you say is the cause of good and evil?[1] The Christian replies, We say that God alone is the cause of all that is good, but not of evil.

The Saracen: What then do you say is the cause of evil?

The Christian: In my opinion it is clearly caused by the devil and by us human beings.

S:　How so?

C:　Through free will.

S:　Have you then free will, and can you act as you wish?

C:　I have been allowed free will in two things only, not in others.

S:　What are they?

C:　If I do what is right,[2] I do not fear the law; rather I am honoured and receive mercy from God. The devil,[3] in the same manner, lured the first man away from God by the free will which was allowed him, and he sinned. He thus lost the station that properly belonged to him. But perhaps you could tell me in turn what things you would call good or evil.

S:[4] The sun, moon and stars are good. You can call these one.

C:[5] That is not what I meant. I was referring to human[6] good and evil: prayer and praise are good, adultery and theft are evil. But if you say that both good and evil are from God, you would make him unjust, which He is not. And if you were to say that God had ordained the adulterer to commit adultery, the thief to steal, and the murderer to kill, they would in that case be worthy of respect for doing God's will. You would thus belie your lawgivers and pervert your Books, since they command that the adulterer and the thief be flogged, and the murderer killed, who should rather be honoured for having done God's will.

S:　Who in your view forms the foetus in woman? (The Saracen evidently poses this problem wishing to demonstrate that God is the cause of evil. For if you were to reply that God forms the foetus in the womb, the Saracen would say, Well, then, God co-operates with fornicators and adulterers. The Christian should then reply as follows:)

C:　After the seven days of creation, there is nothing in Scripture to say that God made or created anything further. If you question this, point to something that He created after that first week (this he cannot do). All things visible came into being during the first seven days, when God also made man and commanded him to procreate. 'Be fruitful, and multiply, and fill the earth' [Gen. 1: 28].

And since man was alive and had living seed, he sowed the seed in his wife. In this way were men begotten, as the Scripture says: Arab begat Seth, and Seth begat Enosh, and Enosh begat Kenan, and Kenan begat Mahallel, and Mahallel begat Enoch.[7] It does not say that God made Seth or Enosh, or anyone else. We thus know that after Adam, who alone was made by God, men were begotten and begat — to this day; and the world goes on by the grace of God. For from that time on, every herb and every plant produced and was reproduced as God ordered: 'Let the earth bring forth grass herbs' [Gen. 1: 11LXX]. By his command every sprouting[8] tree, and herb and shrub, have reproductive powers. And since every herb and plant has in it a living seed, it germinates as it drops to the ground, whether it be self-sown or is sown by another. It does this, not because it is newly created, but in obedience to God's first command. I, too, as I have said, having free will, can sow seed in my wife, or in any other woman, as I wish, and the seed will germinate in obedience to God's first command. This is not because God works and creates each day. For God made heaven and earth in the first week and made the whole universe in six days and rested on the seventh from all His labours, as my Scriptures testify.

S: God said to Jeremiah, 'Before I formed you in the belly I knew you, and I consecrated you from the womb' [Jer. 1: 5 LXX]. Thus he forms all men in the womb.[9]

C: From Adam to our own day, God gave man the power to live and multiply. Adam, as I have said, begat Seth from himself, and Seth Enosh, and every man begats his son in the same way[10] to this day. 'Consecration from the womb' I understand to mean that the children of God have their birth through baptism, as the Holy Ghost testifies: 'But as many as received him he gave power to become the children of God, to those who believe on him, who were born not of blood, or the will of a man, but of God' [John 1: 12].

S: But was there such a thing as Baptism before Christ, and does not Jeremiah predate Christ?

C: The holy apostles bear witness to the fact that some men were baptised in the cloud, and others in the sea [I Cor. 10: 1, 2]. The Lord says in the Gospel: 'Unless one is born of water and the spirit, he cannot enter the Kingdom of God.' This means that even Abraham, Isaac and Jacob, as well as other saints who lived before Christ, only enter the kingdom of heaven and find salvation through baptism. The Holy Spirit confirms this by saying: 'The wicked have gone astray from the womb' [Ps. 58: 3 LXX] — that is to say they are without baptism. This being the case, we aver that all those who are saved owe their salvation to the grace of God through baptism.

S: Are those that do the will of God good or bad?

C: [Recognising his adroitness] I know what you have in mind.

S: Tell me then.

C: You mean that Christ may be said to have suffered willingly or unwillingly. If I say that he suffered willingly, you would retort, Go, then, and prostrate yourself before the Jews for doing God's will.

S: That is what I intended. If you have a reply, let us hear it.

C: What you call 'will' (in the sense of Christ suffering 'willingly'), I call patience and endurance.

S: How can you prove it?

C: From the facts. If you or I just sit or stand, can we do so without God's control?

S: No.

C: If God says, You shall not steal nor commit adultery nor kill, He surely does not wish us to do any of these things.

S: That is so. For if He wanted these things, He would not say, You shall not.

C: Glory be to God! So you admit what I wished you to say: you agree with me that none of us can stand or move without God. And also that God does not want us to commit adultery or steal. If I were now to go and do such things, would you say that God had willed them, or that they occurred because of his tolerance, endurance and patience?

S: [The Saracen sees the point and says appreciatively] This is truly so.

C: You must also grant that God withheld His striking power and endured sin at the cross. In the same way, because He wanted me to repent, He dealt with me as He did with the Jews. For only a few years later, He raised up Titus, Vespasian, and all the Greeks, and put an end to their arrogance.

If the Saracen askes you who was Christ, say to him: 'The word of God.' You may do this without compunction,[11] since the Scripture calls him not 'the Word' only, but also 'Wisdom', 'the Arm' and 'the Power of God', and by many other names. But ask him in turn: What is Christ called in your Scripture? He may then wish to pose another question. Do not reply until he has answered you. He will be compelled to give you this answer: In my Scripture, Christ is called 'Spirit' and 'the Word of God'. Then press him further: Is the Word in your Scripture said to be created or uncreated? If he says 'Uncreated', say to him < Then you agree with me, for God is wholly uncreated. But if he says, The Word and the Spirit are created, then ask him, > [12] And who created the Spirit and the Word of God? And if bewildered he should reply that they were created by God, say: When I said so before, you claimed that it demolished my witness and made all the rest incredible.[13] I will similarly ask you therefore: Was God without spirit or word before he created them? Having nothing to say, he will withdraw.[14]

If the Saracen asks you, Are the words of God created or uncreated? They exchange such arguments with us adroitly to prove that the Word of God (i.e. Christ) was created, which is not the case. If you admit that the words of God are created, he will say to you: You admit then that all the words of God are created. < If on the other hand, you say that they are uncreated, he will say, All the words of God > [15] are uncreated but they are not God. You have thus admitted that Christ, the Word of God, is not God. Do not therefore say 'created' or 'uncreated'. Answer him: I confess only one uncreated Word of God, a hypostasis, as you do yourself also. For I do not call the whole of my Scripture *logia* but *rhemata*.

And if the Saracen asks you, How then does David say: 'The *logia* of the Lord are pure *logia*' [Ps. 12: 7 LXX], and calls them not *rhemata* but *logia*? Tell him that the prophet spoke figuratively not literally. And if he asks you, What is figurative speech and what is literal speech? Tell him that, while literal speech is such proof as is certain and not to be questioned, figurative speech is uncertain proof.

If the Saracen will say to you, Is is possible for a prophet to set forth what is uncertain? Do not hesitate to tell him that the prophets personalise inanimate objects and assign to them eyes and mouths. We thus get, 'The sea saw and fled'. But the sea has no eyes, not being alive. The same prophet speaks of it yet again as if it were alive: 'What is the matter with you sea, that you fled', and so forth. The Scripture (also) says, 'And my sword shall devour flesh', but only a mouth may be said[16] to eat, gorge or drink; a sword cuts but does not devour. Words are thus spoken of as *logia* which are not so.

If the Saracen says to you, How did God descend into the womb? Tell him, Let us use both your Scripture and mine. Your Scripture says that God purified the Virgin Mary above the flesh of all other women, and the Spirit of God and His *Logos* descended on her. My Gospel says, 'The Holy Spirit will come upon you and the power of the

Most High will overshadow you' [Luke 1: 35]. You will thus see that both Scriptures are of one mind and speak with one voice.

I know that when our Scripture speaks of God as descending or ascending, it does so allegorically, not literally. Philosophers speak of a bodily descent and ascent. But God embraces all things and is not confined to any one place. One of the prophets has said: 'Who has measured the sea with his hand, and the heavens with a span, and the whole earth with his fist?'[17] How then can one who holds all things in His own hand be said to descend or ascend?

If you are asked by the Saracen, If Christ is God, how did he eat, drink, sleep, and so forth? Tell him that, according to my Scripture and yours, the eternal, pre-existing *Logos* of God, who created all things, formed the Christ out of the flesh of the pure Virgin Mary to become a perfect man, a living and thinking man who ate, drank and slept, but the *Logos* of God did not eat, drink or sleep, nor was he crucified.

However, you must know that the Christ is said to be double-natured, with one hypostasis. For the one pre-existing *Logos* of God, after assuming flesh, hypostatically not physically, and after the mysterious union with the flesh, did not add a fourth person to the Trinity.

S: Is anything you call divine mortal?[18]

C: The divine is immortal. We trust the Scriptural evidence, for the Scripture has something pertinent to say on the subject.[19]

S: I have received a blow in my flesh, the smitten part suppurates and a worm is formed in the wound. Who created the worm?

C: Give him the answer we have given before, that after the first week of creation of the world, we do not find God making or forming anything whatsoever. But what he ordained and commanded the first week comes to be. However, after the transgression, the earth was[20] condemned to produce thorns and thistles, and for our flesh to corrupt and produce worms to this day.

S: Finally, who in your opinion is greater? He that consecrates or he that receives consecration? You must understand that the question is illusive, so say, I know what you wish to say.

S: If you do, prove it.

C: If I said that it was he who consecrates, you would say to me, Go and prostrate yourself before John the Baptist who baptised and consecrated your Christ.

S: That is what I wished to say to you.

C: Let us make use of an allegory. When you go to the baths with your slave and are washed by him and made clean, who would you say was the greater? The poor slave who is yours by purchase and whose master you are, or you, just washed by him?

S: I would say that I was greater than the one who is my property.

C: I should first give thanks to God before I say that this is how I think of John: a servant rendering service to Christ at the Jordan, where my Saviour was baptised, who there crushed the wicked, demonic heads lying in ambush.

Surprised and bewildered, the Saracen went his way, having nothing more to say.

Notes

1. The Greek adds *aporia*.
2. The Greek has *kaka* instead of *kala*.
3. An unfinished sentence in the original.
4. The Greek text is corrected by Lequienius.
5. Corrected by Lequienius.
6. Corrected by Lequienius.
7. Jared is omitted.
8. Corrected by Lequinius.
9. The Greek text here is somewhat confused.
10. *Na* in the Greek is meaningless.
11. The Greek reads, Do not think you sin in doing so.
12. The words in brackets are taken from the Latin version of Migne's *Patrologia Graeca*, vol. 94, pp. 1586-7.
13. Last word corrected by Lequienius.
14. Four lines left untranslated, for which see Greek text.
15. The words in brackets are from the Latin version of Migne's *Patrologia Graeca*.
16. Read *legetai* in place of *legei*.
17. Greek text has a seemingly redundant line here.
18. Greek text corrupt.
19. Here follows an irrelevant and confused passage in the original.
20. Text corrected by Lequienius.

6 HOW THE QUR'AN INTERPRETS THE BIBLE

Towards a Christian-Muslim Dialogue

Within the general context of Christian-Muslim dialogue, currently much in vogue, it may be relevant to recall the extent to which the Qur'an restates and interprets some of the Bible's major themes. This is a claim the Qur'an itself makes on its own behalf. There is a well-known passage which reads: 'This Qur'an . . . is a confirmation of that which was revealed before it, and an explanation of the Scripture.' (Sura 10: 38)

Clearly, if Christians and Muslims are to understand each other and talk meaningfully to one another, a realisation of the extent of the common ground between them must be an advantage. Attempts at dialogue in the past were bedevilled by a Christian insistence that the Qur'an borrowed heavily from the Bible, and an equally adamant Muslim assertion that Muhammad drew on no source other than divine revelation. To my mind, a more fruitful and less contentious approach lies in drawing attention to the way the Qur'an takes up and expounds some of the central ideas of the Bible. My aim, then, is to bypass altogether the question of the provenance of quranic material and to focus instead on beliefs shared by both faiths. What follows is by no means an exhaustive study; it is rather a preliminary sketch of the subject, written in a spirit of reconciliation.

What is immediately striking on reading both Bible and Qur'an is their agreement on what could be described as the great acts of God: the creation of the world; the choice of Moses as liberator, bearer of revelation and law-giver; the promulgation of the Commandments and the condemnation of apostasy (of which perhaps the best example was the making and worship of the golden calf). Moses looms large in the Qur'an where much is made of the opposition he encountered in his career: evidently the Prophet saw here a parallel with the persecution he himself suffered at the hands of the Meccans and the unbelief he met with.

The God of Creation

The Qur'an, like the opening chapters of the Bible, recounts the wonders of creation. An example may be found in Sura 2: 164:

In the creation of the heavens and the earth; in the alternation of night and day; in the ships that sail the ocean with cargoes beneficial to man; in the water which Allah sends down from the sky and with which He revives the dead earth, dispensing over it all manner of beasts; in the movements of the winds, and in the clouds that are driven between earth and sky; surely in these are signs for rational men.

Significantly, the Arabic word *sawwara*, 'to mould or fashion', of Sura 7: 11, is the exact equivalent of the Hebrew *yasar*, found in Genesis 2: 7, and is the term used for a potter moulding clay. Another philological point may serve to illustrate the underlying similarity. Both Qur'an (S. 2: 189) and Bible (Gen. 1: 14) assert that the role of the heavenly bodies, sun and moon, is to divide up the year and indicate the onset of the seasons. The Arabic word *mawakit*, or 'fixed seasons' is the equivalent of the Hebrew *mo'adim*.

On the subject of the beatific vision, that is to say the sight of God, both Qur'an and Bible agree that it is an experience denied to man on earth. In Exodus 33: 21, the Lord says, 'My face you cannot see, for no mortal man may see me and live.' This admonition to Moses is confirmed in the Qur'an (S. 7: 143) where Moses, communing with God, says: 'Lord reveal Yourself to me, that I may look upon you.' He replied: 'You shall not see Me . . .'

Satan, however, is described somewhat differently in the two texts. The biblical serpent which wrecked havoc in the garden of Eden is represented in the Qur'an not as a reptile but as Satan, a fallen angel (S. 2: 36). Moreover, the Satan of the Qur'an is allowed considerable freedom for evil-doing. In Sura 7: 15, for example, he says to God:

'Because You have led me into sin, I will waylay Your servants as they walk on Your straight path, and spring upon them from the front and from the rear, from their right and from their left . . .'

'Begone!' said Allah. 'A despicable outcast you shall henceforth be. With those that follow you I shall fill the pit of Hell.'

Moses, God's Prophet

The importance ascribed to Moses in both Bible and Qur'an is one of the areas where the two books are most at one. His central role in the Qur'an may be gauged from the fact that he is mentioned no fewer than 196 times as against 96 references to Abraham and a mere 27 to Jesus.

One of the features which distinguished Moses from other prophets was that he was the only one to whom God spoke directly without an angelic mediator, as may be seen from Sura 4: 164 – 'God spake unto Moses, discoursing with him.' This confirms the biblical statements, in Exodus 33: 11 – 'The Lord would speak to Moses face to face, as one man speaks to another' – as well as the striking passage in Deuteronomy 34: 10 – 'There has never yet arisen in Israel a prophet like Moses, whom the Lord knew face to face.'

Starting from this common ground, the Qur'an's claim to confirm and explain the Bible may be seen in the different treatment given by the two works to the story of Moses' survival as an infant. The full narrative in which his mother hid him in a rush basket, where he was discovered by the Pharaoh's daughter, who then entrusted him to a Hebrew nurse who turned out to be his mother, is found in Exodus 2. The quranic account is fragmentary and is more in the nature of an exposition of the story than a recital of it. In particular, the Qur'an makes the point (S. 28: 8) that the Egyptian royal family reared the man who was to be their deadliest enemy. In thus emphasising the intervention of divine providence, the Qur'an provides a commentary on the biblical text.

Another example illustrating the difference in emphasis may be seen in the incident in which Moses killed the Egyptian (Ex. 2: 12 and S. 28: 16). The Bible simply says that Moses, fearing discovery of his action and punishment by the Egyptian authorities, fled to Midian. The Qur'an, however, in a commentary on the story, relates that Moses was filled with remorse at his impetuous act, crying out, 'Forgive me, Lord, for I have sinned against my soul'. This cry of remorse and the declared need for forgiveness have puzzled Muslim commentators as they run counter to the Muslim dogma that prophets are morally impeccable and incapable of crime.

Yet another illustration of the Qur'an interpreting the Bible may be found in the story of Moses' contest with the Egyptian magicians (Ex. 7: 11 and S. 7: 118 and 20: 67). In the Bible, the staves thrown to the ground by the Egyptians turned into serpents just as Moses' rod had done. In the Qur'an, however, the Egyptian magicians are revealed as conjurors: their staves and ropes were made to seem alive (enough to frighten Moses), but this was mere sleight of hand. Moses' staff was able to 'swallow up their false devices'.

Another, perhaps less important, point of quranic exposition may be noted in Sura 2: 57 which reads: 'We caused the clouds to draw their shadow over you.' This may be compared with the 'pillar of cloud' of Exodus 13: 22. However, the physical phenomenon in the Bible is spoken of as a guide to the people by day, whereas in the Qur'an it is more than a guiding cloud, rather a necessary protection from the heat of the sun.

There are areas of similarity to be found in both Qur'an and Bible in the accounts of the events at the foot of Mount Sinai when 'Moses brought the people out from the camp to meet God' (Ex. 19: 17). In the Bible version, the terrified Israelites stood *under (tahtit)* the over-hanging mountain which quaked violently and gave out smoke as if it were on fire. The same word, *tahtit*, is used figuratively in Psalm 139: 15 to mean the 'depths' of the earth, the innermost part, the dark, hidden interior of the womb. The use of this same word in the Mount Sinai episode may have given rise to the rabbinic legend that the mountain was physically raised above the people, arching over them like some huge cask. This biblical version may be compared with the quranic passage (S. 4: 154) where the word *rafa'a*, 'to raise' is found: 'We raised the Mount above them . . .'; and also with another passage (S. 7: 170) which, like Exodus, speaks of a quaking, over-hanging mountain: 'We shook the mountain above them as it were a canopy, and they supposed that it was about to fall on them.'

The Ten Commandments

Scholars have not sufficiently taken note of the fact that the Qur'an provides a version of the Ten Commandments, even through an incomplete one. The principal omission is the command to observe the Sabbath as a day of rest, but, as this was meant for Jews alone, the omission is hardly surprising. Another understandable omission is the biblical instruction to the Commandments: 'I am the Lord your God who brought you out of Egypt, out of the land of slavery.' Indeed, there is little emphasis in the Qur'an on the deliverance of the Hebrews from Egyptian bondage, an event given great prominence in the Bible. Nor do the quranic commandments include the prohibition to take the Lord's name in vain or, in the words of the New English Bible, make 'wrong use of the name of the Lord your God'. To this day in the Middle East, the name of Allah is on every lip, in contexts sacred and profane.

The table below sets out the quranic and biblical commandments side by side for the sake of easy comparison.

Qur'an (N.J. Dawood's trans.)	Bible (New English Bible)	
Sura 17: 23-37	*Exodus 20*	*Deuteronomy/Numbers*
Serve no other gods besides Allah	You shall have no other gods to set against me	
Show kindness to your parents	Honour your father and your mother	A curse upon him who slights his father or his mother (Deut. 27: 16)
Give to the near of kin their due		When one of your fellow countrymen . . . becomes poor,do not be hard-hearted or close- fisted (Deut. 15: 7)
You shall not kill any man whom Allah has forbidden you to kill, except for a just cause	You shall not commit murder	
Do not interfere with the property of orphans	You shall not steal	
You shall not commit adultery	You shall not commit adultery	
Give full measure . . . and weigh with even scales		You shall have true and correct weights and true and correct measures (Deut. 25: 15)
Do not follow what you do not know. Man's eyes, ears and heart — each of his senses will be closely questioned		[Do] not go your own wanton ways, led astray by your own eyes and hearts (Numbers 15: 39)
Do not walk proudly on the earth		Do not become proud and forget the Lord your God (Deut. 8: 14)

The Golden Calf

The story of the Israelites' lapse into idolatry with their worship of
the golden calf provides a further illuminating example of the way the
Qur'an interprets and expounds the Bible. As is explained in Exodus
32:1. the Israelites sought pagan gods because Moses was unduly long

in returning from Mount Sinai. But the Bible offers no explanation for the delay. Not so the Qur'an, which makes clear that the audience with God lasted ten nights longer than was expected: 'And we appointed a meeting with Moses for thirty nights, which we completed with ten other nights, so that his whole time with his Lord amounted to forty nights' (S. 7: 138).

Like the Bible, the Qur'an affirms Aaron's part in the making of the forbidden image. Both accounts also agree that Moses sternly rebuked his brother for this misdeed. But the Qur'an adds the vivid detail that Moses 'threw down the Tablets and, seizing his brother by the hair, dragged him towards him' (S. 7: 150). As in the story of Moses killing the Egyptian, the quranic admission of Aaron's guilt contradicts the later Muslim dogma of a prophet's impeccable moral character — at least with regard to mortal sins.

The Qur'an also sets itself the task of seeking to answer puzzling questions in the Bible, such as why the Law should forbid the eating of such a staple food as camel's meat — the only meat the desert could offer — and similar delicacies. The answer given is that the prohibition was a penalty exacted because of man's sin and disobedience. Sura 4: 159 puts it as follows: 'Because of their iniquity, We forbade the Jews good things [*tayyibat*] which were formerly allowed them: because time after time they have debarred others from the path of Allah . . .' Indeed, quite apart from such detailed explanations, the general display of biblical knowledge in the Qur'an itself noteworthy as may be seen from Sura 45: 16 — 'We gave the Scriptures to the Israelites and bestowed on them wisdom and prophethood'. The Qur'an is thus aware of the three divisions of the Old Testament: the Law, the wisdom literature and the prophetic writings.

A final word may be said about the status of Jesus in the Qur'an. As has already been mentioned, his name occurs no fewer than twenty-seven times but, and this must be counted a crucial difference between Christianity and Islam, he is denied divinity. Nevertheless, he is accorded the highest titles short of being God. He is described in Sura 3: 40 (A.J. Arberry's translation) as follows:

Mary, God gives thee good
tidings of a Word from Him
whose name is Messiah,
Jesus, son of Mary;
high-honoured shall he be
in this world and the next,
near stationed to God.

That the Qur'an should include the 'Word' among the titles of Jesus may be compared with John 1: 1, 'In the beginning was the Word'. Moreover, in a second quranic account of the birth of Jesus (S. 19, entitled 'Mary'), he is referred to as a 'sign' (Arberry) or 'revelation' (Pickthall's translation), in the verse, 'That We may appoint him as a sign unto men and a mercy from Us' (S. 19: 21). The Arabic word *ayah* ('sign') is also used to mean a 'miracle' or, in some contexts, a 'revelatory verse in the Qur'an'. This appellation may be compared with that in Luke 2: 34 (New English Bible): 'This child is destined to be a sign which men reject.' And in yet another instance of similarity with the gospels, Jesus is credited in the Qur'an with the performance of such miracles as giving sight to the blind, healing the leper and raising the dead (S. 3: 49). Some modern Christians might say that this presentation of Jesus in the Qur'an goes more than half way to meeting their own beliefs; although it should be said that nowhere is there a recognition of Christ's redemptive power nor of his revelation of a loving and forgiving God.

For those interested in Christian-Muslim dialogue, these few examples must surely indicate the extent of the common ground between the two faiths. They must also add weight to the Qur'an's claim to confirm earlier revelations and explain the Judaeo-Christian scriptures.

7 THE ETHICS OF MALAMATIYA SUFISM AND THE SERMON ON THE MOUNT

The subject of this essay is not the whole body of the ascetic, ecstatic and mystical movement of Sufism, but only one brand of it which goes by the name of Malamatiya. The famous Cambridge orientalist, Professor A.J. Arberry, spoke rather critically of the Malamatiya. He called them 'drunken Sufis' and described their movement as 'extravagant antinomianism'. In other words he accused them of bypassing the law for their own ends. I think this accusation somewhat unjust. If it applies to the movement at all, it does so only after it had degenerated. Only at that late stage did the Malamatiya court contempt and give people reason to despise them by infringing the law. To return to Arberry's description, he says that they were an 'extremist sect who held that the true worship of God is bestowed by the contempt in which the devotee is held by his fellowmen'.[1] In Hosea's time, people said, 'The prophet is a fool; the man of the spirit is mad' (Hos. 9: 7), and St Paul, as we know, was told by Festus, the Roman governor, that he was mad.

Who were the Malamatiya? From where did they derive their name? It is a puzzling word. The root meaning is *lama*, 'to blame'. But who was to blame? Who passed judgement? And why the notion of blame? It cannot refer to their judging others as this was against their principles. They believed that it was wrong ever to blame anyone. It is, therefore, more probable that they acquired the name because they were always blaming their own carnal self, *nafs*, and were always trying to repress it. The self was their great enemy, the object of their censure and of their constant vigilance. They were an inward-looking sect, highly critical of themselves, always on the lookout for lapses: the self had to be subdued, humiliated and punished at all costs. It was a cunning creature, forever setting traps and seeking to snare them — hence the need for watchfulness. In short, they were greatly preoccupied with their own vices, not with those of others.

The main source of information about the Malamatiya is an eleventh-century Arab writer from Nishapur, Persia, Abu 'Abd al-Rahman al-Sulami, who died in 1021. He divides learned and pious men into three groups.[2] The first are the legal experts who devote themselves to jurisprudence, collecting laws, preserving and teaching them. They are scholars in what al-Sulami calls exoteric learning — that is to say public, external knowledge, in contrast with the hidden, esoteric mysteries known only to a special elite. This first group busies itself with the Qur'an and tradition: it comprises, in fact, the classic *'ulama.*

The second group is more of an elite. Al-Sulami calls its members *ahl al-ma'rifa* and describes them as 'special' people *khawass,* to whom God has vouchsafed special knowledge of Himself. They turn their back on life and give themselves up wholly to God and to His commandments. They are innocent of the good things of life and do not hanker after them. Their chief and only concern is God who has given them the distinction of being able to perform miracles, *karamat.* These 'special' people have privileged access to unseen mysteries but their external behaviour is, nevertheless, conformist: they comply with the outward requirements of the law.

Al-Sulami's third and most exclusive group are the Malamatiya — the recipients of God's special favours. They are near Him and in union with Him, a supreme distinction for Muslims who believe in a transcendent deity. It is such praise that is almost un-Islamic. Al-Sulami insists on this notion of connectedness with God. The Malamatiya, he says, have been allowed to penetrate and experience the secret of union. Their whole inner being is directed towards intimacy and nearness with God, while their outer life is lived in strict conformity with the law. They live, therefore, a sort of double life, on two planes. Al-Sulami attributes to them the best of both these worlds: they abide by the law but also enjoy this extraordinary privileged union with God. It is worth remarking that, whereas Arberry accuses the Malamatiya of disregarding the law — of antinomianism — al-Sulami is their apologist, claiming that their two lives, the inner and the outer, do not impinge on each other and are not in competition. They represent the summit of what al-Sulami admires, the peak of religious and mystical experience. It is as well to remember that this Sufi historian was the teacher of al-Qushairi (d. 1074).

There are many questions concerning the origins of the Malamatiya which need further study and clarification. We are not sure, for instance, who was and who was not a Malamati. We know, however, that the movement flourished in and around Nishapur in the second half of the third Hijra century. We also know that Abu Hafs al-Haddad (d. 260) and Hamdun al-Qassar (d. 271) were the earliest Sufis to propagate Malamati ideas. Two others who must have played an important part are Ahmad ibn Khidruya (d. 240) and Abu 'Uthman al-Hiri (d. 298).[3]

Al-Sulami pursues his description of this special elite by listing what he considers to be their chief rules or articles, forty-five in number. These articles do not represent a systematic code — they are not a carefully thought out body of doctrine. Indeed, they contain many overlapping ideas. But they are a statement, diffuse and repetitious perhaps, of their moral and spiritual ideal. To us they are of special interest because they have much in common with the Sermon on the Mount. I would not suggest that there is perfect identity or that there are not important differences. What they have in common is a moral ideal far surpassing that by which we run our lives. It is not my present intention to boost Islamic Sufism nor to prove how close the ethics of the Malamatiya are to those of the New Testament. Nor is it my intention to demonstrate the moral superiority of the teaching of Jesus. My only objective is to draw attention to a little known phase of Sufism.

As will be seen, there are some striking parallels between the ethics of the Malamatiya and the ethical teaching of Christ and I should like readers to note similarities of language as well as of ideas. Often, however, while the prescription may be the same, the reasons advanced for persuading us to adopt it are different, and these differences betray a profoundly different view of morality.

Let us consider some specific issues. In each case I shall quote relevant passages from the forty-five Malamatiya articles and from the Sermon on the Mount or other gospel passages. (My biblical quotations are from the New English Bible.)

Poverty, Humility and Service

Both the Malamatiya and Jesus preach a philosophy of humility and service, and both urge us not to set our hearts on riches. But the reasons underlying these recommendations are far apart. For the Malamatiya, the carnal self is the great enemy, and humility is prescribed the better to crush him. For Christ, humility is advised because all men are one in the sight of God. The self should not be crushed but should find fulfilment in the service of others.

To quote a few examples. In article 31, the Malamatiya declare that to show great concern for earthly good is a sign of future perdition, whereas trust and serenity are indications of future bliss. Jesus said, 'How hard it will be for the wealthy to enter the kingdom of God' (Mark 10: 23); he also said, 'Blessed are you poor' (Luke 6: 20).

In article 23, the Malamatiya say that poverty is a virtue if it is a secret known only to God. To let your poverty be known is to be a beggar, of which there are many. In article 41, the Malamatiya add that a man should let his house speak for him at his death: it should be like the houses of the pious men of old. These sentiments strongly resemble Matthew 6: 19: 'Do not store up for yourselves treasure on earth.'

On the subject of service, the Malamatiya display their usual self-denial. In article 32, they declare their dislike of being waited upon or of being paid homage. They claim to be servants and slaves, not deserving of such consideration. For the Christian version we have the well-known statement of Jesus in Mark 10: 43f: 'Among you, whoever wants to be great must be your servant, and whoever wants to be first must be the willing slave of all.'

In article 44 — one of their most characteristic principles — the Malamatiya declare that one should only accept help if one is thereby humiliated. Nowhere is their hatred of the self more evident. In article 9, they urge the believer to conceal his true character, and particularly his glorious intimacy with God, and only expose those features which are likely to lower and humble him in the eyes of others, to court contempt and rejection. Jesus also recommends meekness : 'Blessed are the meek', he said in Matthew 5: 5, but there is no hint in his prescription of the masochism and self-flagellation of the Malamatiya.

Social Relations

In article 34, the Malamatiya prescribe that the believer should serve as a light to his fellow men at night and as a staff on which to lean by day. There is an obvious parallel here with Matthew 5: 14, 16: 'You, like the lamp, must shed light among your fellows . . .'

In articles 25 and 28, the Malamatiya recommend that the believer should not concern himself with the vices of others as his own are sufficiently preoccupying. In the same vein, Jesus asks in Matthew 7: 3: 'Why do you look at the speck of sawdust in your brother's eye with never a thought for the great plank in your own?'

In article 6, the Malamatiya tell the believer to be civil to those that treat him rudely; to treat others with respect; to make excuses for other people; to be kind, and not to do to others as they do to him. This compares strikingly with Matthew 5: 44-7: 'Do good to those who hate you . . . If you greet only your brothers what is there extraordinary about that?'

In article 3, the Malamatiya urge us to give others their rights without claiming our own. Jesus takes the same line in Luke 6: 30: 'When a man takes what is yours, do not demand it back.'

Prayer and Good Deeds

Another characteristic feature of the Malamatiya is the extreme nature of their views on petitionary prayer. Here, too, they are merciless with themselves. In article 29, for instance, they declare that God should not be petitioned except in case of dire necessity. The believer should come to God broken in spirit, in a state of bankruptcy, with no claim on God or man . . . Only then is his petition permissible and may he expect an answer. Jesus, too, discouraged useless reptition in prayer, but his whole attitude was welcoming. 'Ask and you will receive,' he said. 'Seek, and you will find; knock and the door will be opened. For everyone who asks, receives . . .' (Matt. 7: 7, 8).

In contrast, the Malamatiya seem positively afraid of receiving an answer. In article 43, they express their distress when their petitions are answered, fearing it be a trap to lure them to destruction.

They are closest to the teaching of Jesus in their views on merit and good deeds. In article 27, they hold that only an ignorant servant will presume to deserve God's gifts. Indeed, they believe that to have any knowledge at all is to recognise that all we receive from God is undeserved. In support of this view, the Malamatiya quote a tradition according to which the Prophet declares that no one shall enter paradise through good works. When someone asked him, 'What, not even yourself, Apostle of Allah?' he replied, 'Not even I.' A fair parallel is Luke 17: 10 – 'when you have carried out all your orders, you should say: "We are servants and deserve no credit. We have only done our duty." '

The Problem of Evil

When the Malamatiya come to deal with the problem of evil they appear to be in full agreement with New Testament teaching on the subject. Indeed, or this point, it is fair to say that they depart from orthodox Islam, even though they seek to bolster up their doctrinal position with quranic support.

The doctrine they teach is that Man's *nafs*, his carnal self, is rebellious, ignorant, hypocritical and conceited. It is wholly evil. It should be held in the greatest suspicion and should be the object of the greatest vigilance. The Malamatiya quote five passages from the Qur'an to prove their case: In three of these passages, man is declared to be rash and hasty and fretful from birth – literally from his creation (Suras 17: 11/12; 21: 3; 17: 18/19). In a fourth passage, Sura 100: 6, man is declared to be ungrateful. The Arabic term *kanud* also means rebellious. But the key passage, with which the Malamatiya made great play, is Sura 12: 53 – 'Surely the *nafs* incites man to evil.' This is the verse of the Qur'an in which the Malamatiya find the fullest justification for their doctrine. It also explains the puzzle of their name: the 'blameworthy', as the historian al-Sulami makes clear. If the Qur'an itself paints the *nafs* black, describing it as evil, then it fully deserves to be blamed. Hence the name Malamatiya.

The doctrine of human corruption is clearly brought out in four of the Malamatiya articles. Article 7 runs: They accuse or censure the self at all times . . . it rarely earns their approval or sympathy. Article 8 holds that the conceit of the self ever lures it to destruction. The same notion is expressed in article 13: The ultimate goal of knowledge is to think well of God and to think ill of the self. Finally, article 19 says that man must be the enemy of his carnal self and never commend it. This view of human sinfulness is very close to what Jesus taught. In Matthew 7: 11 he declared: 'If you then, who are evil . . .' It is the word 'evil' we should note. And again, in Matthew 19: 17: 'Good?' said Jesus. 'Why do you ask me that? God alone is good.'

The Spiritual Anatomy of the Malamatiya

We must next consider what overall view of the structure of man emerges from Malamatiya doctrine. What is the composition of man or, in other words, what is man's spiritual anatomy? The Malamatiya see man as divided into four distinct compartments, arranged on a descending scale.

At the summit is the Spirit, *ruh*, or source of life. To reach this summit is to enjoy union with God, the supreme goal of every Sufi. The climb is long and arduous but the objective sublime.

Just short of the summit is another compartment which the Malamatiya call *sirr*. This is the secret ethical core of man, the spring of his moral behaviour. It is a shade below the spirit, but shares with it a vision of the unseen mysteries of the Godhead.

Lower still lies the heart, *qalb*, which, according to the Malamatiya, is the repository of both knowledge and emotions. This is the motor of everyday life. It is on this level of human achievement that man runs the risk of setting himself up as a co-creator with God.

Finally, and right at the bottom, crouches the familiar beast, the *nafs*, the carnal self — source of all evil, Satan's workshop. In Malamatiyan doctrine, man either climbs towards the summit or descends to the beast.

We find in al-Sulami an account of a spiritual journey undertaken by a famous Sufi, Abu Yazid al-Bistami (d. 875). For twelve years he wrestled with the carnal self. For five more years he fought the heart. And one whole year was spent in the difficult passage from the self to the heart. Then he perceived that he was bound by a girdle within him which impeded his spiritual progress. For five mcre years he laboured to sever it. Then came revelation when, breaking free, he saw the world of men around him as so many corpses. They were all dead and he read funeral prayers over them. *Allahu Akbar*. There is an echo of this notion of the world being spiritually dead, but not knowing it, in the Qur'an (S. 16: 21): 'Dead, not alive, and are not aware . . .' In the Gospels, we find Jesus saying in Matthew 8: 22: 'Let the dead bury their dead.'

The Malamatiya also describe their spiritual anatomy in the following terms. At the peak is the realm of spiritual ecstasies. To descend from it to the realm of the secret ethical core and to reveal the secrets of the spirit is to open the door to hypocrisy. To descend further to the heart, and to reveal the secrets of the ethical core, is to throw open the door to idolatry. To sink still further to the level of the carnal self is to reduce the whole of man's spirituality to chaff blown about by the wind.

Hypocrisy

Of all the characteristics of the carnal self, the Malamatiya were on special guard against hypocrisy. Their rules contain many injunctions against making a display of acts of worship, of good deeds, of learning or of poverty, or indeed of their special relationship with God – that is to say of their ecstatic states. All had to be concealed and ruthlessly played down. This exceedingly humble attitude was justified by reference to a general principle: that nothing good and praiseworthy done by man was his own. It was the agency of God working in him.

Jesus, too, as we know, was equally severe on the question of hypocrisy. In Matthew 6: 1 he declared: 'Be careful not to make a show of your religion before men . . . do not announce your acts of charity with a flourish of trumpets as the hypocrites do . . . When you pray do not be like the hypocrites who love to say their prayers . . . for everyone to see them . . . When you fast, do not look gloomy like the hypocrites . . .' We find very similar views in the principles of the Malamatiya. Their very first article, for example, is that it is idolatrous to make a display of acts of devotion or to parade one's ecstatic states. Similar injunctions against hypocrisy and undue display are found in article 23, which says that poverty should be kept secret, article 24 which says that a Sufi should not make himself conspicuous by dressing in rags, and in article 26 which says that acts of charity should be inconspicuous.

Conclusion

I have tried to present a glimpse of the moral and spiritual ideal of the Malamatiya. The reader will have noticed some striking parallels with the Sermon on the Mount. Like the teaching of Jesus, their doctrine is not a cut-and-dried ethical code, nor is it a comprehensive system of philosophy. What is wholly admirable about their system is that it represents a break-away from Islamic legalism. Indeed, so little do they insist on the outward and meticulous observance of the law that some of their critics, as we have seen, accused them of antinomianism. Like Jesus, the Malamatiya had a perception of man's fallen nature and his essential sinfulness. Their whole system was designed to correct and reform him.

There is, however, one vital difference. As I see it, Jesus sought to recreate man in God's image. 'You must therefore be all goodness just as your Heavenly Father is all goodness' (Matt. 5: 48). He sought to set up a kingdom of righteousness and peace — a heaven upon earth. 'Set your mind on God's kingdom and his justice before everything else' (Matt. 7: 33).

As we have seen, the greatest concern of the Malamatiya was to attain union and communion with the truth — God. This was the moral and spiritual ideal for an elite. Indeed, they were a self-conscious minority, separate not only from the *'ulama* but from other Sufis as well. However close, therefore, their ethics may seem to the Sermon of the Mount, they are different in having no message for the multitude. They were concerned only to save themselves. Lastly, the Malamatiya set as their highest goal the spiritual ecstasy of union with God. They say nothing about loving God, but they come very close to what Jesus named the second greatest commandment: Love thy neighbour as thyself.

The Forty-Five Articles of the Malamatiya as recorded by Al-Sulami[4]

1. They consider it idolatrous to make a display of their acts of devotion; to parade ecstasy is apostasy.
2. They refuse gifts which do them honour, preferring to beg in humility; there is no glory in servitude.
3. They give others their rights without claiming their own.
4. They submit only to force, yielding wealth and property under pressure, like a miser. This they do, not to allow the self (*nafs*) to take pride in generosity.
5. They believe that they would be objects of contempt — more to blame than to praise — if their deeds and mystical attainments

were open to public scrutiny.

6. They are civil to those that treat them rudely; they are forbearing and deferential; they make excuses for others; they are kind and do not do to others as they are done by.

7. They believe that they must constantly suspect the carnal self (*nafs*), whether it advances or falls behind, whether obedient or disobedient; it rarely earns their approval or sympathy.

8. They hold that the conceit of the self ever lures it to destruction; it must therefore be carefully watched.

9. They conceal their true character, exposing only those features which are likely to lower and humble them in people's eyes; they court rejection in order to preserve their outer and inner peace. They disclose their separation from God rather than their union with him.

10. They are set against taking pleasure in pious deeds; this they consider deadly (for the soul).

11. They extol God's work in them, but make little of their acts of obedience.

12. They also hold it like a principle that their soul is not their own but God's purchase, as it is written: 'God has bought from the believers their selves and their possessions against the gift of Paradise' (S. 9: 12).

13. They hold that the ultimate goal of knowledge is to think well of God and to think ill of the self.

14. They prescribe instruction by a spiritual director (*imam*) whose guidance should be sought in all matters pertaining to knowledge and mystical experience (*ahwal*).

15. They believe that those works or deeds which one notices and approves of are for that reason worthless and unacceptable; the high and unseen are alone acceptable.

16. They make a point of noting their own shortcomings and excusing those of others.

17. They hold that the heart should be properly focused on God; that there should be good relations with our fellows while life lasts (*waqt*); and that we should keep secret any bestowal of grace.

18. They hold that the essence of servitude is two-fold: to feel acutely our need of God and to follow closely the example of his apostle.

19. They believe that one should be the enemy of one's carnal self and never commend it.

20. They believe that to admire one's own work betrays a shallow and frivolous nature; how can one boast about things which are ours

only on loan?

21. They believe that scientific questions should not be made a subject of discussion, nor something to boast about, nor should one reveal God's secrets to the unworthy.

22. They hold that listening to music is only permissible if it makes for reverence and is unaccompanied by shaking and shouting.

23. They believe that poverty is a virtue if it is a secret known only to God; to reveal one's poverty is to leave the company of the faithful and become a mere beggar of which there are many.

24. They believe that they should not dress differently from others but should resemble them in outward appearance.

25. They believe that they should not concern themselves with other people's vices — their own are sufficiently preoccupying; they should be vigilant regarding the evils of the self and seek to reform it.

26. They believe that he who gives should not make much of his gift, seeing that he only bestows what God has entrusted to him; and the recipient is entitled to it.

27. They hold that only an ignorant servant will presume that his acts and obedience secure God's gifts as if merited. To attain to any knowledge at all is to recognise that all we receive from God is pure favour and is undeserved.

28. They believe that a man should not gaze at his brother's vices except with the object of concealing them.

29. They believe that God should not be petitioned except in case of dire need, when one is nothing and has nothing, with no claim on God or man. He will thus come back to God weak and broken in spirit, with no good deeds or mystical experiences; he will come like a bankrupt having let go of everything; only then is his petition permissible and may then expect it to be heard.

30. They believe that the inertia (*ghafla*) which follows a period of work and strain is an act of mercy which is sent to us by God to comfort and refresh us.

31. They believe that great concern for earthly goods is a sign of future perdition, just as quiet trust in whatever has been ordained is an indication of future bliss.

32. They dislike to be waited upon, to be revered, and for people to do them homage. Such things are for free men, not slaves.

33. They hold that a believer should guard against his own clairvoyance (*firasa*) and should never claim that power.

34. They hold that a believer should be light for his brethren at night

and a staff to lean on by day.

35. They believe that if a man is possessed of much learning his works are few; if he has but little learning his works are many. (I asked Abu Hafs for an explanation and he said: A man of great learning makes little of his many works knowing their inadequacy, whereas a man of little learning rates his petty works highly, unable to see their blemishes and inadequacies.)

36. They believe that the evidence of the ear should not be set above that of the eye; that is to say, that the praise one hears must not get the better of what one sees and knows of the self and its failings.

37. They believe that one should avoid discussing the finer points of the sciences and learned allusions, nor seek to plumb depths, but to adhere to the bounds of command and prohibition.

38. They interpret trust to mean to recognise God as the only overseer, sustainer and witness.

39. They believe that signs and wonders (*karamat*) should not be divulged; they are to be looked upon as possible traps to lead one away from God and into perdition.

40. They believe that one should restrain one's tears when listening to music, at a *dhikr*, or at a learned discourse; one should preserve a sombre mien. Abu Bakr al-Makki said: The reward of weeping is the pleasure that goes with it. Abu Hafs permitted tears caused by remorse. Abu 'Uthman, who opposed it, said: To cry is in fact to be comforted; it is permitted, however, when it crushes the spirit and ravages the body.

41. They believe that one should let his house speak for him at his death — this is preferable to pleading poverty when alive — so that at the time of death your house will be like that of the pious poor of old.

42. They believe that one should not ask for help from a fellow creature, for that means seeking help from one who is himself in need; his need, unknown to you, may be greater than your own.

43. They are sad and depressed when their petitions are answered, fearing it be a trick to lure them to destruction.

44. They hold that one may accept aid if it is humiliating to do so, but should reject it if it exalts one and satisfies one's natural greed.

45. They define true friendship as giving generously to your brother from what you possess but not coveting what is his; to grant him his rights but not to demand yours; to defer to him rather than he

to you; to bear his discourtesy without being rude to him; and to make much of small favours you may receive from him and make little of any you may render.

Al-Sulami ends his record with a quotation to the effect that if another prophet were to arise among men – an eventuality precluded by Muhammad being the seal of the prophets – he would surely be a Malamati.

Notes

1. A.J. Arberry, *Sufism. An Account of the Mystics of Islam* (London, 1956), pp. 70, 74.
2. Abu 'l-Ala 'Afifi, *Al-Malamatiya* (Cairo, 1945), pp. 86-7.
3. Al-Qushairi, *Al-Risala* (Cairo, n.d.) pp. 17ff; Abu 'l-Ala 'Afifi, *Al-Malamatiya*, pp. 33-9; R. Hartmann, 'Al-Sulami's Risalal al-Malamatija', *Der Islam*, VIII (1918), 157-203.
4. This translation is an abridged version of the original. Care has been taken not to omit anything essential.

8 AN ARAB'S CONCERN WITH LIFE AFTER DEATH

Arab concern with the after-life has passed through three well-defined stages. In the earliest, or the pre-Islamic pagan period, Arabs grieved at the loss of blood relations and friends and sought comfort in the thought that the deceased were not really far away. They believed that the departed lived a life of their own and enjoyed a conscious existence in the grave. A similar belief was nurtured by the ancient Hebrews, who knew the abode of the dead as Sheol, or Hades. Job says:

> If only thou wouldst hide me in Sheol
> and conceal me till thy anger turns aside,
> if thou wouldst fix a limit for my time there, and then remember me!
> Then I would not lose hope, however long my service,
> waiting for my relief to come.
> Thou wouldst summon me, and I would answer thee;
> thou wouldst long to see the creature thou hast made.
> [Job 14: 13-15]

Pagan Arabs cared for their dead and supplied them with food and drink, which was also the practice of the ancient Hebrews until it was banned by the Mosaic law (Deuteronomy 26: 14). In Arab society, friends and relatives kept in touch with the deceased, lingered at the burial place, and even pitched a tent at the graveside; they could not tear themselves away. Coming upon the grave of an acquaintance, they would call his name and greet him: the deceased was believed to return the greeting. Owls fluttering around were thought to be the spirits of the departed, and their screeching was taken to be the moaning of the dead. The spirit was also referred to as 'echo', 'skull', or 'soul'.

Layla al-Ahyaliya, the poetess, on a visit to the graveside of her poet-lover, dared question the belief that the deceased returned one's salutations, despite the fact that her lover had himself said so in one of his poems. At this bold denial, an owl appeared and flew straight into her face. Layla dropped dead (Al-Aghani, x, 82; Hamasa 576).

The pagan Arab refused to allow death to sever the ties of blood or friendship: following the bier, he would cry: 'Do not be far away!' Besides food, he would also provide the deceased with a riding camel which was tethered at the graveside and left there to die without food or water. In later Islamic times, after this practice was officially banned, its occasional continued observance was justified by the need to provide the deceased with a riding camel at the resurrection. However, while the pagan pre-Islamic Arabs believed in survival, they knew nothing of the resurrection of the body.

In the second stage, that is to say after the emergence of Islam, Arabs continued to believe that the departed lived their own life in the tomb, but interest now centred on man's destiny and ultimate condition. The two articles of faith that the prophet Muhammad tried to convince his fellow Arabs of were, first, that there was going to be a day of resurrection; the pagan Arab found it difficult to believe that God would 'gather his bones', and 'shape again his fingers': (Qur'an 75: 4). 'They shall say, "What, are we being restored as we were before? What, when we are bones old and decayed?" ' (Qur'an 79: 10). Muhammad's second article was that there was going to be a day of judgement — that man was accountable to a sovereign creator who had 'not created the heavens and the earth and whatever is between them in sport ... but for a serious end' (Qur'an 44: 38). The free-living Arab, be he nomad or sedentary, boggled at the thought of being called upon to give an account of his faith and deeds.

The pagan Arab spoke unashamedly of the things that for him made life worth living: to spring upon his favourite mare on an early morning raid; to outmanoeuvre his complaining women folk and quaff sparkling red wine with boon companions; to bet in a game of chance; and to be closeted with a girl on a rainy day (see Tarafa's *Golden Ode* for three out of the four just mentioned). This accountability must have been as unpalatable as was the alms tax, prescribed in the Qur'an, which had to be reimposed on the Arabs by force of arms after the Prophet's death.

The underworld, as revealed by Muhammad in the Qur'an, was no longer the habitat of beings who were mere shadows of their former selves; it was now full of life and movement: a sad place for some, a happy one for others, depending on the life they had lived above, and the God they had believed in or denied. However Muhammad's moral tone was not lost on the Arabs. The Qur'an speaks of the great divide between the 'people of the right hand' and the 'people of the left':

What! have we not made him eyes
and tongue and lips,
and guided him to the two highways?
Yet he attempted not the steep.
And who shall teach thee what the steep is?

It is to ransom the captive,
or to feed in the day of famine
the orphan who is near of kin, or the poor that lieth in the dust,
Beside this, to be of those who believe, and enjoin steadfastness on
    each other, and enjoin compassion on each other.
These shall be the people of the right hand:
while they who disbelieve our signs,
shall be the people of the left.
Around them the fire shall close.

                    [Qur'an 90: 10-20] [1]

The Qur'an is the best source for the second stage of the Arab's concern
with life after death. Dalton Galloway ('The Resurrection and Judgement in the Qur'an')[2] affirms that the last day, or the day of resurrection and judgement, was always in Muhammad's mind and on his tongue,
so much so that he coupled the belief in the last day with the belief in
Allah, and it was the 'obsession' which he communicated to his followers
and companions. The term *al-'akhira*, the 'hereafter', occurs 113 times
in the Qur'an. The great day is called by many names and locations
including 'the day when the leg shall be bared', implying that on that
day people will cast dignity to the winds and tuck up their ample outer
garment to run faster. The happenings of the great and terrible day will
begin with a shout and a blast of the trumpet. This summons to judgement will bring together not only all humans but also the *jinn* and the
animal creation. Every creature's work will then be placed on the
scales to be weighed. He whose balance is heaped up with good works
will be admitted to the garden, but he who shows a light balance and
few merits will be sent down to the pit. Hell will be full to overflowing
as more and more people are thrust into it, and no pleading will be
permitted.

No! I swear by the Day of Resurrection . . .
What, does man reckon We shall not gather his bones?
Yes indeed: We are able to shape again his fingers,
Nay, but man desires to continue on as a libertine,
asking, 'When shall be the Day of Resurrection?'

                    [Qur'an, 75]

The Blow! What is the Blow?
The day that men shall be like scattered moths,
and the mountains shall be like plucked wool-tufts.

Then he whose deeds weigh heavy in the Balance   shall inherit a
    pleasing life;
but he whose deeds weigh light in the Balance shall plunge in the
    womb of the Pit.
And what shall teach thee what is the Pit?
    A blazing Fire!

[Qur'an 90: 10-20]

Galloway rightly says that 'no revivalist preacher has excelled the
Prophet in dangling an audience over the terrors of the future torments'.
It appears, however, that as Islamic *sunnah* ('tradition') grew and expanded in the centuries that followed Muhammad's death, new horrors were
added which the Prophet never conceived. I am referring to the interrogation in the grave and the torments that follow. There were now to be
two trials: one in the grace when a person died, the other at the end of
the world. The underworld was peopled with angels and demons of
various kinds. The angel of death, whose work it was to extract the soul
from the dead body, had two eyes, one in his face, the other in the
nape of the neck. He showed himself to the dying, seized their soul
without a moment's respite and left the house amidst the piteous
cries of the family. Islamic tradition has a good deal to say about the
interrogation in the tomb and the resulting treatment meted out to
believers and infidels. The virtuous man is welcomed by angels 'with
faces like to the sun', the unbeliever is received by angels that are ugly
and revolting. There is silk and musk for the believer, sackcloth and live
coals for the infidel. The believer's tomb automatically turns into a
verdant garden, the infidel's tomb is full of seven-headed snakes.
     Al-Ghazali faced critics who questioned the existence of such snakes
in the tomb. It was plain, they said, from an examination of an infidel's
tomb that there were no snakes there, much less the seven-headed
variety. Al-Ghazali retorted:

We are dealing with the unseen world. The snakes and scorpions of
the tomb are not of the same species as the snakes and scorpions of
our lower world; they belong to a different species and are perceived
by a different sense of sight. Muhammad's companions failed to see
the angel of revelation who came to him, yet they believed the truth
of the revelation. We also know that suffering may be of the mind,
as is the case when one dreams that he has been stung and cries out
in his sleep. Then again, a man may be tormented by the loss of his
worldly goods to which he is much attached. These forms of torment

are possible and real. The mind, unlike the body, suffers no change at death and the deceased retains consciousness; he may therefore suffer pain or enjoy felicity, as the case may be.[3]

The Two Examining Angels

Tradition has much to say about Munkar and Nakir, the two black angels who interrogate the dead regarding their faith and works. The believer's answer works miracles, causing his dark and narrow tomb to become spacious and full of light. The infidel's answer has the reverse effect: the tomb closes in on him so as to bruise his ribs. He is put in the charge of a brute that can neither see, hear nor speak; it wields its iron whip and never pities its victim.

A tradition which goes back to the Prophet's favourite wife, A'ishah, says that the tombs of Zaynab, the Prophet's daughter, and that of Sa'd b. Mu'adh, a prominent companion, were miraculously widened and made comfortable. This gratified the Prophet and lit up his face.

The Great Day of Judgement

At the blast of the trumpet, the graves will open and the dead will rise. They will be led naked to the great meeting-place — a vast plateau in a depressed desert plain, unlike any place on earth because the earth itself will have been changed beyond recognition. The crowded mass of creatures, gathered from the seven heavens and the seven earths, together with angels, *jinn* and devils, will stand in the blazing sun, finding no shade anywhere. Sweat pouring out of them will flow like so much water reaching up to the knee, the hip and even higher. There they will stand for God knows how long.

The Portents

On that day, tradition relates, the heavens will be rent, the stars scattered, the twinkling luminaries murky, the sun veiled, the mountains levelled. Camels, ten months gone with young, will remain unattended, while the seas boil and hell stokes up its fires. On that day each soul will see what it sent forward and what it kept back. Balances will be set up, books opened and hell brought near. The fire will crackle and the infidels will despair. At the interrogation, people will be questioned about both great and trivial things. Prophets and apostles will be asked if they delivered the message. Hell will boil and seethe finally to engulf those who dared disobey the Most High.

The Bridge (Qur'an 37: 23)

The bridge that stretches across the fiery pit is sharper than a sword's edge and finer than a hair. The upright will run across in safety. Some will walk across, others will just manage to crawl across, still others, labouring under a load of guilt, will slip and fall into the pit. The Prophet will be the first to reach the other side. His prayer will be: 'Preserve us, Oh Lord!' Angels will rescue believers who are too frightened to step onto the bridge, and will help them make their way across through the leaping flames.

The Intercession (Qur'an 93: 5b)

In one tradition, the Prophet is reported to have said: 'Five things were given to me alone out of all God's prophets: I was feared by the people who lived as far as a month's journey from where I was. I was allowed to keep the spoils when others were not. My people were allowed to worship anywhere and everywhere. I was sent not to one people but all peoples. I was given the prerogative of interceding for others.' When all intercessors fail them, they will come to Muhammad and ask him to intercede for them in their plight. The Prophet will approach the throne and bow down before the Most High. God will then say what he has not said to anyone before. 'Rise, Oh Muhammad, ask and you will receive, plead and your pleading will be accepted.' The Prophet will say: 'My people, I pray for them.' The best of them will then enter a door on the right, while others will enter by a common door. The good folk and the learned will be allowed to intercede for their own tribe and their household. If one of God's people was in life given a cup of cold water, he will be allowed to plead for his benefactor, rescuing him from Hell. Another tradition runs: some of the Prophet's companions spoke with admiration of Abraham, the friend of God, of Moses, who conversed with God, of Jesus, God's Word and Spirit. Muhammad said: 'All you say is true, and I, without boasting, am the beloved of God whose intercession will be accepted on the Day of Judgement.'

The Pool (Qur'an 108)

Kawthar is a river of Paradise, its water is whiter than milk, sweeter than honey and more fragrant than musk. Its banks are of gold, the river bed is of pearls and coral. One tradition says that the domes on each side of the river are of hollow pearls. The Prophet's pool, which is a part of the river, is supplied with water from Paradise. To drink of this water is never to thirst again.

Hell

The Qur'an and the traditions refer repeatedly to the pit. The Qur'an says:

> Not one of you there is, but he
> shall go down to it; that for the Lord
> is a thing decreed, determined.
> Then we shall deliver those that were
> Godfearing; and the evil-doers We shall
> leave there, hobbling on their knees.
>
> [19: 73, 74]

The condemned will cry out to Malik, their keeper, but in vain. There they will lie, manacled, with fire above them and fire below them, fire on their right and fire on their left; their clothing is fire and so is their bedding. Pierced by many sword thrusts, their foreheads broken, their livers ruined, their flesh, skin and hair gone, they will be given new skins periodically for their torments to begin all over again.

> Surely those that disbelieve in our signs —
> We shall certainly roast them at a fire; as often
> as their skins are wholly burned. We shall
> give them in exchange other skins, that they
> may taste the chastisement.
>
> [Qur'an 4: 56]

Gehenna is the highest of Hell's several compartments; the others follow in descending order: Hell-Fire, the Flame, the Scorcher, the Blazes, the Inferno and the Abyss, which is bottomless. Muhammad's companions, startled on one occasion by a terrific crash, were told that it was the sound of a falling rock which had been let down into the pit seventy years earlier and had only then touched bottom.

The vehemence of the fire is described in these words: God, the Most High, ordered the fire to burn for a thousand years till it turned red, then another thousand till it turned white, and yet another thousand till it turned black, its present colour. When the fire complained that it was being consumed, the Lord gave it two natures: in the summer it is boiling hot, in the winter it is freezing cold. The Qur'an speaks of the drink offered to the wicked:

> . . . Then was disappointed

every forward tyrant — beyond him Gehenna,
and he is given to drink of oozing pus,
the which he gulps, and scarcely swallows,
and death comes upon him from every side:
and still beyond him is a harsh chastisement.

[14: 19, 20]

Punishment, however, will be in proportion to a person's wrong-doing: 'God shall not wrong so much as the weight of an ant' (Qur'an 4: 44a).

Heaven

Al-Ghazali exhorts believers to meditate in fear on the terrors of Hell, and likewise recollect and look forward to the promised blessedness of Heaven. The radiant citizens of Heaven sit on thrones beside rivers flowing with wine and honey, and are refreshed with perfumed wine. They have for companions youths and wide-eyed houris untouched by men or *jinn*. Here the citizens are kings, denied no pleasure. At the daily audience round the throne, the inmates will be rapturous over the beatific vision.

Al-Ghazali says: 'If Heaven were nothing more than a life without accidents and privations, without sickness or death, that would be reason enough for giving up this world for the sake of the next.'[4]

A tradition traced back to the Prophet says: 'If you want to enjoy wine in the hereafter, abstain here and now. This applies equally to gold and silver ornaments and silk garments: shun them in this life and you will have them in abundance in your eternal home. The clothes of the citizens of Heaven never wear out and the person himself never grows old. We shall experience what eye has not seen, what ear has not heard, and what has not entered the mind of man.'

When the Prophet was asked if the clothes above were hand-woven or created, he replied that they grew on trees. The food of Heaven is manna, fattened birds, quails, milk and honey. One will only have to look at a bird in the sky and desire it, for it to drop at one's feet, roasted and ready for the table. The main dish will be the flesh of the bull that has been grazing in the gardens of Eden. The organism will dispose of body wastes by means of perspiration exhaled like musk.

Traditions explained quranic verses relating to life in Heaven: for example, the meaning of 'wide-eyed houris, restrained in tents' (55: 72) is that these females are never angry and never go away. They are spoken of as 'pure spouses' (Qur'an 3: 13) because they are free from excretions of any kind. The expression 'occupied rejoicing' (36: 5b) means that men will be occupied deflowering virgins (Ihya', vol. iv, p.508). We learn that the inhabitants of the Garden will be fair, beard-less, curly-headed, eyelids darkened with antimony, thirty-three years of age and ninety feet tall.

A tradition found in both Al-Bukhari and Muslim declares that the greatest delight awaiting the citizens of Heaven will be to look on the face of God. This is named the 'surplus' (Qur'an 10: 27), as it will be granted the virtuous over and above their reward. Jarir b. Abdullah said: 'We were sitting with God's Messenger (May the blessing and peace of God rest upon him) when he saw the full moon. He said: "You will see your Lord as you see this moon and will come to no harm. This beatific vision is dearer than all else." '

Statistics

The Qur'an refers to 'charming abodes in the Gardens of Eden' (61: 12). These abodes, tradition affirms, are pearly palaces: each palace contains seventy courts, each court seventy houses, and each house seventy couches, with a houri on each couch. There is a tree in the Garden through whose shade one may ride for a hundred years without crossing it. The smallest house in the Garden has a thousand servants, each going about his appointed task. Finally, everyone in the Garden will marry five hundred houris, four thousand virgins and eight thousand non-virgins.

Notes

1. *The Koran*, trans., J.M. Rodwell (1909).
2. Dalton Galloway, 'The Resurrection and Judgment in the Qur'an', in *Moslem World*, vol. 17 (1922), 348.
3. Virginia Cobb's trans. Al-Ghazali, *Dhikr Al-Mawt Wa-Ma Ba'duh Kitab Al-Aghani.*
4. Al-Ghazali, *Ihya, 'Ulum al-Din* (Cairo edn.), vol. iv.

9 THE GLOSSES IN THE BOOK OF GENESIS AND THE J-E THEORY

An Attempt at a New Solution

In the course of translating the Book of Genesis into colloquial Arabic three things came to my mind in quick succession: first, I was struck by what I later came to believe was a stylistic principle with the writer, namely, his frequent use of synonyms and glosses; second, this led to the idea that the duplication of the divine name in the text could only be another example of this principle; and third, the recognition then followed that, if this view were correct, it would prove upsetting for the J-E theory and its variants which, basing themselves on the use of two divine names in the biblical text, Elohim and Jehovah, and on other internal evidence, dispute Mosaic authorship of the Pentateuch and seek to identify older underlying source documents.

The story of the French eighteenth-century physician, Jean Astruc, father of the two-document theory, as well as the consequent labours of Bible scholars and critics, and their elaborate subdivisions of the text of the Pentateuch, is too well known to need retelling here. It was an endeavour which reached its climax in Julius Wellhausen's famous book, *Prolegomena to the History of Ancient Israel*, first published in 1878 but still a powerful influence on Old Testament scholarship. However, regarding this theory of source analysis as a whole, it may be worth quoting Professor E. Robertson: 'When you subdivide your main documents into two, three, four, or more "hands", the disintegration of the theory comes perilously near.'[1]

I wish in this essay to confine myself mainly to the linguistic side of the question, leaving aside the issues of date, authorship or historicity of the book in question.

From a long acquaintance and study of the Hebrew text, I have come to believe that a possible explanation of the puzzling use of the names of God by the writer of Genesis — he uses now one name, now another, and in places both names together — may be found in his singular method and way of writing. We find him making liberal use of glosses and circumlocution: he has a way of putting two synonymous words side by side with or without a conjunction; he says the same thing three times, using each time a different, but synonymous word;

and he repeats things sufficiently explained already with every new person introduced (to show how the things mentioned affect that particular person). It is this peculiar style which, I believe, has not been sufficiently taken note of by scholars. In particular, the bearing of this stylistic oddity on the use of the names of God and on the so-called duplicate accounts of the stories of creation, the flood, the birth of Isaac, and so forth, has not been adequately considered.

Why does the writer make such liberal use of glosses? It is not, I think, because he is verbose, or because of some peculiar idiosyncrasy, nor is it oriental exuberance. Rather, I have come to believe that he writes as he does out of sheer necessity, He is writing not only for a people and a nation, but for a mixed multitude (Ex. 12: 38 and Nu. 11: 4). Moreover, the people are themselves a great mixture: they are of Bedouin origin, Aramean domicile, Egyptian upbringing and Canaanite connections. Glosses and explanations, together with an extensive use of words taken from Arabic, Alladian, Aramaic, and Egyptian, are for such a mixed audience an absolute necessity.

Glosses and Synonyms

A striking example of the writer's style may be found in Genesis 1: 11 where a fruit tree is explained as a tree bearing, or rather making, fruit; one would think that a 'fruit-tree' was self-explanatory, but the writer evidently does not think so. However, the expression is not repeated in v.12, where he speaks of a tree making fruit, but not of a fruit tree.[2] Another example is in Genesis 6: 21: 'All food that is eaten.' We would tend to consider redundant the words 'that is eaten', but the writer seems to use them as a gloss for the Hebrew *ma-akhal*. We have a third example in Genesis 11: 30: 'Sarah was barren, she had no child.' The writer is here evidently explaining the Hebrew word *'aqarah*, in addition to telling us about Sarah's childlessness. A fourth example is from Genesis 6: 17: ' . . . I do bring the flood of waters upon the earth.' 'Flood', or rather 'the flood', is not in construct with the following word in the genitive, but is in the absolute state. Here again, the writer is apparently explaining the word *mabul*[3] to his readers.

The following glosses tell the same story: Genesis 1: 11 gives two synonymous words for grass — *deshe* and *'esebh*, which stand together without a conjunction; they do not stand respectively for 'tender grass' and 'herbs' as some commentators would have us believe, because one of the synonyms is left out from v.29.[4] Another pair is found in Genesis 1: 24 — *nefesh* and *haya*, translated 'living creature'. Here, too, one of the words is left out from v.28, which proves them synonymous.[5]

This is also the case with *tzelem* and *d'muth* in v.26, translated 'image' and 'likeness', although one is left out from v.27. Another example comes from Genesis 9: 2 – *mora-akhem we hitkhem*, translated 'fear' and 'dread'; in this case, too, only one of the pair is mentioned in Genesis 35: 5. Another pair is *ger* and *toshabh*, a 'sojourner' and a 'dweller' in Genesis 23: 4. Another pair is *saq* and *amtahath*, translated 'sack', occurring in Genesis 24: 27. Yet another example is *rahat* and *shoqeth*, meaning a 'watering trough' in Genesis 30: 38. They are placed together in the plural without a conjunction, but only one of the synonyms is used in v.4, and they are never used together again. One last example is *lotesh* and *horesh* of Genesis 4: 22, which have been variously translated as 'hammerer and artificer' or 'forger of every cutting instrument', or as 'whetter or instructor of every artificer'. The old Aramaic paraphrase *Onkelos* recognises the two words as synonymous; *horesh* alone is used in later scripture for an artisan.[6]

Other pairs found in the text include *tohu-bohu*, translated as 'waste and void' (Gen. 1: 2); *kotz we dardar*, translated as 'thorns and thistles' (Gen. 3: 18); *na' we nad*, translated as a 'fugitive and wanderer' (Gen. 4: 14); *nin we nekhed*, translated as 'offspring and posterity' (Gen. 21: 23). These can hardly be alliteratives since they do not recur in twos again in simple prose narrative.

A gloss which clears up a very difficult passage is to be found in Genesis 49: 4: 'For thou wentest up to thy father's bed, then thou profanedst my couch *'alah.*'[7] The word *'alah*, following the word 'couch', cannot mean 'he went up' or 'which he went up', as this would involve a harsh transition from the second person to the third. My view is that *'alah*, juxtaposed to *y'zu'ah* ('couch'), may well be a gloss meaning 'bed'. *'Alat* means a resting place on some Phoenician gravestone inscriptions, where it is even placed side by side with *mishkabh*, a word also found in the Genesis passage.[8]

Another example of an unrecognised gloss which has caused difficulties for translators is to be found in Genesis 16: 12 where Ishmael, in the English versions, is much maligned by being described as a 'wild ass among men' or a 'wild ass of a man'. The Hebrew text has two words juxtaposed *pere*, 'wild ass' and *adam*, 'man'. In the tribal culture of the time, a 'wild ass' was a laudatory appellation, a by-name for a chief, or leader, or tribal head. What the angel told Hagar was that her son, Ishmael, was destined to become a great man. The gloss *adam*, 'man', was no doubt added at some point for the benefit of sedentary readers who had moved a long way from nomadic life and who might themselves have been puzzled by reference to a wild ass.[9] The gloss makes clear that the reference is to a man not to an animal.

Yet another example of a misunderstood gloss may be found in Genesis 21: 20 where Ishmael is described as *robhe qashshoth*, sometimes translated as: 'He became, as he grew up, an archer.' J. Skinner, in his commentary on Genesis, remarks that: 'The syntax is peculiar, the growing up has already been mentioned.' The puzzle is cleared up when the two juxtaposed words are seen as synonyms. *Qashshoth*, judging by its form, means not an 'archer' but a 'maker of bows', an honourable profession since the making of suits of armour is ascribed in pre-Islamic Arabian poetry to both David and Solomon. *Robhe*, in turn, from *rabha*, 'to shoot',[10] could mean either a 'shooter', or, as is more likely, one that makes shooting instruments. The two cognate Arabic words are *qawwas* and *barra*. Indeed, the Arabic *bara*, 'to make an arrow', is a metathesis of the Hebrew *rabha*.

The Divine Names

We are now in a position to deal with the duplication of the name of the deity in Genesis 2: 4. There can be no doubt that 'Jehovah' as a name is newer than 'Elohim' or than 'El Shaddai', the Almighty. We are told so very plainly in Exodus 6: 3 — 'And I appeared unto Abraham, unto Isaac, and unto Jacob, by the name of God Almighty, but by my name Jehovah was I not known to them.' The fact of its being a newer name would of itself be a sufficient reason for not using it alone, at least not at first. So, the writer does here what we have seen him do in other passages, namely he juxtaposes the new word with the older Elohim. It is significant that this usage is first found in Genesis 2: 4, in the section beginning, 'These are the generations [literally begettings] of the heavens and of the earth when they were created . . .' This verse may originally have stood at the beginning of the book, because it is one of the formulae, of which there are ten altogether in Genesis, which serve as a framework for the whole book.[11]

Linguistically, the name 'Jehovah' derives from *ehyeh*, 'I am' (Ex. 3: 14): the verb in the first person singular, as uttered by God, becomes a proper name when changed into the third person singular. Thus *ehyeh* becomes *Yahweh*, just as *odeh*, 'I praise', spoken by Leah, becomes Judah or Yehudah (Gen. 29: 35). The different names of God have widely different connotations as may be seen from the theophanies in which they occur. His manifestations as El Shaddai were sudden, momentary and overwhelming, 'an horror of great darkness' as in Genesis 15: 12, or 'an overpowering of the overpower' *(k'shod mishaddai)* in Isaiah 13: 6. As Jehovah, in contrast, he was an ever-present God who dwelt among his people.

Does the statement of Exodus 6: 3, quoted above, rule out the possibility that the same writer may have used the name Jehovah in the story of the patriarchs? This need not be the case, since the writer habitually uses new place-names before relating the events which bring about the change of name. There is, for example, his early use of Zoar, in Genesis 14: 2, which was the name given later in Genesis 19: 22 to one of the doomed cities after it was saved from general destruction. The writer deals with this place-name as he does with the names of God: he puts the city's old and new names together, 'Bela which is Zoar', although he also uses Zoar by itself, without explanation, even before the event, as in Genesis 13: 10.

The writer of the Book of Judges acts in the same way when relating the story of Gideon, whose name was subsequently changed to Jerubaal. He first uses both names together, with an explanation: 'Jerubaal, who is Gideon' (Judges 7: 1); he then goes on calling him Gideon, but also 'Jerubaal, son of Joash' (8: 29); only in one passage does he put both names together, calling him Jerubaal Gideon (8: 35).

One last example is from the story of Jacob who was sent off to Padan-Aram to stay with Laban, the Aramaean (Gen. 28: 2, 5, 6). This place is later referred to simply as Padan (48: 7), and later still as just Aram (Num. 23: 7). I think it would be fair to conclude that here, too, we have an old and a new name which are first used together, the one supplementing the other, until the old is dropped.

The Critics' 'Selected Lists of Expressions'

In the critical analysis of the Genesis documents, the critics make use of 'Selected lists of expressions which are highly characteristic of J and E respectively'.[12] For example, the two Hebrew words used to describe the destruction of the flood victims, *gav'u* and *metu*, translated as 'expired' and 'died', are brought forward as proof of literary discontinuity, and indicative of the work of two authors and of two different accounts. 'Expired' of Genesis 7: 21 is ascribed to E, while the second word, 'Died' of v. 22, is ascribed to J. The critics have failed, however, to account for a third word or expression, 'blotted out', in v. 23. How arbitrary such analysis is may be seen from Genesis 25: 8 where three different words and phrases for dying are used in just one verse: 'Then Abraham gave up the ghost [literally expired], and died in a good old age, an old man, and full of years; and was gathered to his people.' To quote another example of critical analysis, the two synonyms for 'young', *tza'ir* and *qatan*, are ascribed respectively to J and E, and yet both words are found in that part of the story of Joseph which Dr Driver ascribes to J (Gen. 43: 33 and 44: 12).

A third example comes from the story of Abraham where two words are used for a 'maid-servant'. So, one of them, *shifhah*, of Genesis 16 is ascribed to J, while *amah* of Genesis 21 to E. And yet both words are used together in the story of Jacob and Rachel in Genesis 30: 3, 4.

A fourth example is taken from the story of Joseph where two expressions, *beth sohar*, 'prison', and *mishmar*, 'ward', are ascribed to J and E respectively. However, a third word used in the story, namely *bor*, a 'dungeon', is ignored. Two synonyms for 'dry land' — *harabha* and *yabasha* — are likewise assigned to J and E respectively.

It seems certain that the use of different words for 'maid', for 'dying', for 'prison' and for 'young' is no more than a writer's literary device. We find him doing the same thing in the story of Isaac (Gen. 26), where two different words are used for 'digging a well' — i.e. *hafar* and *khara;* two words also for an 'oath' — *alah* in v.28 and *sh'wu'ah* in v. 31: two words for 'overtaking' — *hissig* and *hidbiq* (Gen. 31: 23, 25); two words for the 'pieces of a carcase' — *b'tharim* and *g'zarim* (Gen. 15), the former word is here used in the singular, whereas the plural is found in Jeremiah 34: 18. Two words are used for 'paying a visit' — *avar'al* (Gen. 18: 5) and *sur el* (Gen. 19: 2); two words for 'window' in the story of the flood — *tzohar* and *halon* (Gen. 6: 16 and 8: 6); three different expressions are used in the same story to describe living beings — 'all flesh', 'all in whose nostrils is the breath of life' and 'all living things' (Gen. 7: 21 f). And lastly, two words are used for 'creating' in Genesis 1 — *bara* and *'asah* — while a third, *yatzar*, in chapter 2 is rightly used for shaping man out of clay, a word also used by Jeremiah to describe the work of the potter (Jer. 18: 2).

All we have said leads to the conclusion that the Book of Genesis has been somewhat misunderstood and misjudged by those Bible scholars and critics who built up elaborate theories regarding the authorship of the work which they ascribed to an array of writers and redactors. We have tried to show that the key to the Book, missed by many critics, lies in the writer's peculiar style and method, in his use of glosses, explanations and repetitions. With this linguistic key in hand, I feel that we can speak more reassuringly about the unity and antiquity of the first book of holy scripture, and the oldest prose work in the Hebrew language.

Notes

1. E. Robertson, *The Old Testament Problem: A Re-investigation* (1950).
2. C.J. Ball, in *The Book of Genesis: Critical Edition of the Hebrew Text* (1896), deletes 'fruit' from Gen. 1: 11 because he could not explain it.
3. Kittel, in *Biblica Hebraica,* tries to smooth over *mayim,* and offers *mi-yam* as an emendation.
4. J. Skinner, *Genesis* (International Critical Commentary), p.23: 'It is impossible to define them [i.e. *deshe* and *'esebh*] with scientific precision.' In Gen. 1: 30 we have the gloss *yereq* instead of *deshe,* where Skinner remarks: 'These linguistic differences are sufficient to prove literary discontinuity of some kind' (p. 35).
5. J. Skinner, *Genesis* (I.C.C.), p.27: This 'has all the awkwardness of a gloss'.
6. *Lotesh* later came to mean a sharpener or polisher of swords, clearly the work of a sword-maker.
7. 'Not very acceptable rendering of this difficult clause has been proposed' — Skinner, *Genesis* (I.C.C.), p.515.
8. Cf. M. Lidsbarski, *Ephemeris für Semitische Epigraphik,* iii, p. 286.
9. See M.S. Seale, 'Arabic and Old Testament Interpretation' in *The Expository Times,* lxvi (December 1954), p. 92; and M.S. Seale, *The Desert Bible.* pp. 88-9.
10. *The Gesenius Hebrew-English Lexicon,* p.916.
11. S.R. Driver, in *An Introduction to the Literature of the Old Testament,* p. 6, says: 'The narrative of Genesis is cast into a framework, or scheme, marked by the recurring formula, "These are the generations".'
12. J. Skinner, *Genesis* (I.C.C.), p. xlix.

10 OUTSTANDING PASSAGES IN QUR'AN AND BIBLE

Are there passages in the Qur'an that are finer than others? And can some be described as only second best? Ibn Taimiyya (d. 1326), the great Hanbalite theologian, defends this point of view, selecting certain commanding passages for special praise in a way which we might today find instructive.[1] Earlier Muslim thinkers such as Al-Ash'ari (d. 936) and Ibn al-Baqillani (d. 1013) argued that to set one quranic passage above another was to cast aspersion on the Word of God. Al-Ash'ari held, for instance, that to maintain that: 'some passages were superior suggested that others, lacking that superiority, must be inferior or deficient; the Word of God cannot be dissected. Superlatives such as *afdal* and *a'zam* stand for *fadil* and *'azim*.'[2] He meant that superlative forms had to be taken as having only a positive sense.

To answer these objections, Ibn Taimiyya draws support from a passage by Al-Ghazali (d. 1111):

> If the light of reason will not let you see the difference between the throne verse [S. 2: 56] and other verses dealing with debit and credit; and if you cannot differentiate between Sura 112, the Chapter on Unity, and Sura 111, the imprecation upon Abu Lahab; and if your soul, obsessed by tradition, is afraid to entertain such a difference, follow the lawgiver (God's blessing and peace be upon him) who said: 'Sura 39, *Ya Sin,* is the core of the Qur'an: the first Sura, the *Fatiha,* is the most excellent of all the Suras; the throne verse [S. 2: 256] is mistress of all other verses; and Sura 112, Unity, is tantamount to a third of the Qur'an.'[3]

Ibn Taimiyya turns to the Qur'an itself for further support, quoting Sura 2: 100: 'Whatever verse we cancel or cause thee to forget we bring a better or its like.' This passage, he argues, means that: 'God declares that a verse may at times be replaced by a similar one, or it may, on some other occasion, be replaced by one superior; this goes to prove that some verses are alike, others superior.'[4] In another context, Ibn Taimiyya makes much the same point by remarking that a verse which has been abrogated or set aside is replaced by another which is better.[5]

But it is the story of Joseph in Sura 12: 3 — 'One of the best of narratives *[ahsan al-qasas]* ' – which stimulates Ibn Taimiyya to set out his ideas at length. The argument he outlines is also most revealing of the workings of his mind.

He begins by making clear that, to describe the story of Joseph as 'the best' is to say no more than that it is the best of its class.[6] It is well known, he argues, that the story of Moses and Pharaoh is finer and nobler by far. Also much finer are the stories of other prophets and apostles, such as Noah, Hud, Salih and Shu'aib, which is the reason they are recounted more than once in the Qur'an, whereas the story of Joseph occurs only once. There is no comparison, he maintains, between Joseph's predicament and that which befell Moses, Noah, Abraham and the others. The latter suffered great persecutions, they were more favoured by God and attained a higher rank. They won greater victories. Noah, Moses, Abraham and Christ called upon men to worship but one God and were, on that account ill-used. They suffered because they chose to worship God, freely accepting suffering for His services and for His love. They would not have suffered had they not believed and had they not called others to His worship.

Joseph's case was different. He was parted from his father, and suffered from that, but he had no choice. But even without drawing any outside comparison, Ibn Taimiyya sees a difference between Joseph's imprisonment for refusing to sin and the patience he displayed when ill-treated by his brothers. The first was finer and more praise-worthy.[7]

Writing almost two centuries later, Al-Suyuti (d. 1505) devoted a special section of the *Itqan* to a discussion of the difference between excellent and superlative in the Qur'an. He cites pious forbears for the view that just as the Sura of Unity (S. 112) was the finest of Suras, so the throne verse (S. 2: 256) was the finest of verses. It is, says Al-Munir, the only verse in which God is mentioned seventeen times by name, epithet or pronoun, expressed or understood.[8]

These then were the superior passages of the Qur'an for pious men who knew what and why they believed. What faith have we to match theirs? And what, if any, are our superior passages?

This writer was told of a present-day Muslim who quoted with feeling and pride the following verse from the Qur'an: 'The East and West are God's: therefore whichever way ye turn, there is the face of God' (S. 2: 109). Muslims and non-Muslims alike will join in admiration for a truth so beautifully expressed. A Christian rejoinder might well be to quote the words of Jesus to the Samaritan woman who anxiously enquired where the right *Qibla* might be: 'Neither on this mountain nor in Jerusalem . . . God is spirit and those who worship him must worship in spirit and in truth' (John 4: 21, 24).

The following quranic passage will no doubt rank high for many:

> God is the light of the Heavens and of the Earth. His light is like a niche in which is a lamp − the lamp encased in glass − the glass, as it were, a glistening star. From a blessed tree it is lighted, the olive neither of the East nor of the West, whose oil would well nigh shine out, even though fire touched it not! It is light upon light, God guideth whom he will to His light, and God setteth forth parables to men, for God knoweth all things. [S. 24: 35]

This splendid passage may be matched by Psalm 27: 1 which has given comfort to many a Jew and to many a Christian:

> The Lord is my light and my salvation; whom shall I fear? The Lord is the stronghold of my life; of whom shall I be afraid?

To which a Christian might add the Master's self-disclosure:

> I am the light of the world; he who follows me will not walk in darkness, but will have the light of life.

The notion of God's unity came to the pagan Arabs with the blinding light of revelation, satisfying a great need. We, too, today stand in urgent need of God's light to guide us in the conduct of our affairs. many of us, the supreme passage will remain:

> For God so loved the world that he gave his only Son, that whosoever believes in him should not perish but have everlasting life.
>
> [John 3: 16]

A Biblical Proof Text in Al-Ghazali

More than half a century ago, D.B. Macdonald expressed his high regard for al-Ghazali's gifts as a writer and theologian, and even more for his spiritual liveliness. This is how he put it:

> Al-Ghazali, by training a theologian and lawyer, bridged the widening gap, took over mysticism with its intuitionalism and spiritual life into the dry body of theology, and gave the Church of Islam a fresh term of life. It is this spiritually real and living side of his character and work that constitutes his abiding interest for us.

Other theologians of Islam are important as links in an historical chain; he, in virtue of what he was in himself, of the conversion he went through and the experience he had.[9]

I should like in this section only to examine the use made by al-Ghazali of a biblical text which he unquestioningly accepted as a Prophetic tradition and even, possibly, as a sacred tradition since it is prefaced in some manuscripts by 'God said . . .'.[10] The verse in 1 Corinthians 2: 9 (RSV), runs as follows:

But as it is written, What no eye has seen, nor ear heard, nor the heart of man conceived, what God has prepared for those who love him.

The verse occurs three times in al-Ghazali's *Tahafut al-Falasifa (Refutation of the Philosophers)*, and once in his *Al-Madnum bihi 'ala ghayri ahlihi* (That which is to be withheld from the Unworthy).[11] It first appears in a shortened form in the opening invocation of the *Tahafut*. There, al-Ghazali prays that, after escaping from the wails of the day of resurrection and on entering the delectable garden, God may grant him 'What eye has not seen, nor ear heard, nor entered the heart of man'.[12]

The verse occurs again in chapter XX of the *Tahafut*, where al-Ghazali is concerned to refute the philosophers' rejection of the resurrection of the body, the sensuous delights of Paradise and the notion of a physical Hell. In discussing this theme, what is significant is that al-Ghazali approves the philosophers' preference for spiritual rather than sensual pleasures and quotes the verse in I Corinthians in support.

He notes that the pleasures of revenge or victory are often preferred to those of food, drink and women; similarly, a man might abstain from food for a whole day if engrossed in the pleasure of a game of chess or backgammon. The philosophers were right, he says, to maintain the superiority of angels over animals, seeing that the latter only enjoy physical pleasures. He concludes as follows:

The spiritual pleasures of the after-life are therefore superior to the pleasures of this life. If it were not so, the Prophet would not have said, 'I have prepared for my righteous servants what eye has not seen, nor ear heard, nor entered the heart of man.' And God said, 'No soul knows what refreshment He has in store for them.'[13]

Thus al-Ghazali seeks to refute the philosophers by rehabilitating the sensual delights of Paradise while at the same time approving the philosophers' order of preferences. Once more he refers to the biblical text: 'The existence of the more refined pleasures does not rule out the other kind. It is more proper to accept them both, seeing that both are promised us.'[14] He returns to the argument in the *Madnun,* drawing support once more from Corinthians both for the credibility of the notion of sensual pleasures in Paradise and for the diversity of tastes which will there be catered for:

> Thus, if one should dream of lush vegetation, a gushing stream and a beautiful face; rivers flowing with milk, honey and wine; trees bedecked with jewels, sapphires and pearls; gold and silver palaces; couches with precious stones and handsome youths to wait on you. Such a dream would mean different things to different men and would be differently interpreted. To some it might represent the joy of learning and discovery; to others governance and authority or to crush an enemy; to others again it might represent the joy of seeing friends. There are different categories as there are different tastes with different persons. The same applies to intellectual plea- sures. And if we are told, 'What eye has not seen, nor ear heard, and has not entered the heart of man' — it means that all these things are within the bounds of possibility. It is possible that one and the same person will enjoy all these things, or that every person will get what he is in a position to enjoy. A person, obsessed by tradition, who concretizes these pictures and sensuous pleasures, knowing nothing of gnosis and mystical experience, will have what he has concretized. The gnostics, however, who despise sensuous pleasures will be intro- duced to the finer intellectual delights which are more to their taste and for which they are craving. Paradise is so constituted that every person will find in it what he desires most.[15]

A brief word in conclusion. Al-Ghazali insists that we must believe that which is written, but, in extolling the superiority of spiritual delights, he finds support in a verse from the Bible. Paradise, for him, is not pearly gates and golden streets (Rev. 21: 21), nor wide-eyed houris (Qur'an 37: 48), but a new heaven and a new earth. I feel sure that he would have heartily endorsed St Paul's other dictum that the sufferings and indeed the pleasures of this world are not to be compared with the glory which awaits us (Romans 8: 18).

Loads and Fetters (Qur'an 7: 156)

One aspect of the 'new teaching'[16] which Jesus introduced into Roman Palestine dealt, mundanely perhaps, with food. We sometimes forget to what extent the food habits of the Jews were, as they still are for very many, bound within a strict framework of taboos and prohibitions. Jews in Arabia, for example, were forbidden to eat camel's meat — a grave disability, seeing that this was a staple food in the desert; the fatty hump was looked upon as a special delicacy. The prohibition, of course, stems from Leviticus 11: 4.

Intent upon easing these disabilities, the Qur'an offers some relief. There is a telling passage (in Q. 7: 156) in which Muhammad, described as the Prophet of the common folk, [17] initiates some dietary reforms, 'making lawful for them the good things *[al-tayyibat]* and relieving them of their loads and fetters *[aghlal]* that were upon them'.

It is certain that the *tayyibat* did not include the blood-cake, made from blood drawn from a live camel and mixed with coarse flour before baking. But the relief Muhammad offered was at any rate only partial since pork remained prohibited. The commentaries remain silent on the question of what exactly the permitted delicacies were and say nothing about blood-cakes, although these must have been very common indeed.

Some clues to the importance of food taboos in the new community which grew up around the Prophet are to be found in an account of a debate which I take from al-Wahidi.[18] Muhammad was confronted by some of his Jewish critics who contested the claim that he professed the faith of Abraham. They asserted that this could not be the case, seeing that he ate camel's meat and drank camel's milk, both forbidden in the Law. Muhammad replied that no such prohibition existed in Abraham's day, but they insisted that it dated back as far as Noah.

The issue was settled by a quranic revelation which ran: 'All food was lawful to the children of Israel before the Law was given, except what Israel forbade for himself' (Q. 3: 88). This made it quite clear that there were no food prohibitions before Moses, and therefore none in Abraham's day.

Al-Wahidi affords us another example of the binding nature of food taboos. He cites the case of the celebrated 'Abdallah ibn Salam and his friends who were converted from Judaism to Islam and yet abstained from eating camel. When fellow Muslims remonstrated with them, Abdallah referred them to the Law.[19] These episodes give us an insight into the cramped, taboo-ridden society against which Jesus's new teaching was directed. His words seem no less than a declaration of liberation:

'Listen to me, all of you, and understand this: nothing that goes into a man from outside can defile him; no, it is the things that come out of him that defile him . . . Thus he declared all foods clean.'

When the disciples asked Jesus to explain his disturbing doctrine, he said: 'It is what comes out of a man that defiles him. For, from inside, out of a man's heart, come evil thoughts, acts of fornication, of theft, murder, adultery, ruthless greed and malice; fraud, indecency, envy, slander, arrogance and folly, and they defile the man' (Mark 7: 15-23).

There is a vivid account in the Acts of the Apostles in which Peter is seen wrestling with food taboos. One day, at noon, he went up on to a roof to pray, and, feeling hungry, wanted something to eat. This is how the story is told:

While they were getting it [the food] ready, he fell into a trance. He saw a rift in the sky, and a thing coming down that looked like a great sheet of sail-cloth. It was slung by the four corners, and was being lowered to the ground. In it he saw creatures of every kind, whatever walks or crawls or flies. Then there was a voice which said to him, Up, Peter, kill and eat. But Peter said: No, Lord, no; I have never eaten anything profane and unclean. The voice came again a second time: It is not for you to call profane what God counts clean.
[Acts 10: 10-15)

Scholars have often drawn attention to the contrast between the yoke of Jesus which is easy to bear, and the taboos and restrictions of the Pharisees which were 'grievous to be borne' (Matthew 23: 4). But Jesus offers us much more than freedom from dietary restrictions. He offers to make every man a child of God and raise him to a position in which questions of food and drink appear trivial and petty. This is what he tells us about yokes and fetters: 'Come to me, all whose work is hard, whose load is heavy, and I will give you relief. Bend your necks to my yoke, and learn from me, for I am gentle and humble-hearted; and your soul will find relief. For my yoke is good to bear, my load is light (Matthew 11: 28-30).

The Missing Chapter

It is a pity that Chirstians know little or nothing of the story of Jesus as related in the Qur'an. The quranic account is not only of great intrinsic merit, but it is also part of our common heritage which it would be wrong to neglect. And yet there seems to be something lacking in the portrait of Jesus which emerges from the Qur'an. As one puts together the disparate elements spread over several Suras, the picture seems shadowy and incomplete: we are left with a Christ who is enigmatic and puzzling. It is as if there were a missing chapter in the account.

One cannot hope to do justice to such a theme in a brief note; my object here is merely to advance a few thoughts to ponder over in a spirit of sincere enquiry.

From the outset we encounter something baffling: the very name of Jesus in the Qur'an — *'Isa* — is not one we easily recognise. It bears little resemblance to *Yasu'*, the name found in Arab Christian tradition. The letter *'ayn* in 'Isa is found at the beginning of the word, whereas in Yasu' it is at the end. It is clearly not the Arabic equivalent of the Hebrew *Yeshu'a* or *Yehoshu'a*. More serious still is the fact that in 'Isa we miss the derivation *yasha'* of the original, which means 'to deliver'. How central is this root meaning may be seen from Matthew 1: 25 — 'Thou shalt call his name Jesus, for he shall deliver his people from their sin.'

While on this theme of derivation, we might also note that, in a number of places in the Qur'an, Jesus is referred to as *Masih*, the Arabic equivalent of 'Messiah', although meaning nothing comparable. Commentators of the Qur'an have advanced many different explanations of the meaning of *masih*, many of them far-fetched. For example Al-Baidawi's commentary on the quranic verse, 'Mary, God gives thee good tidings of a Word from Him, whose name is Messiah, Jesus, Son of Mary', runs as follows:

> Messiah is one of his illustrious titles; the Hebrew original is *Mashiah*, that is to say the blessed one. It is derived from *almash*, meaning either that he was blessed, or that he was cleansed from sin, or else that he travelled across the world, or that he was anointed by Gabriel.

The fact that al-Baidawi advances no fewer than four different explanations suggests his uncertainty about the real meaning of the word. In the original language of the Bible, *mashah* means to anoint for kingship or for the priestly office, and hence an appropriate title for the Messiah.

Another title which is frequently given to Jesus in the Qur'an is *Ibn Maryam*, the 'Son of Mary'. We cannot quarrel with this appellation, particularly since the Qur'an vigorously defends the Virgin's chastity. But we keenly miss any reference to Jesus as the Son of Man, found so repeatedly in the synoptic gospels. This title, which Jesus used of himself, is important because of the insight it gives us into Jesus' consciousness of himself as Messiah. He clearly saw himself as the Son of Man spoken of in Daniel 7: 13, 14, or as the one endowed with power who was to come again in glory as in Matthew 26: 64.

The Virgin Birth is a dogma which is repeatedly upheld in the Qur'an. And yet we find there is no explanation for the miraculous birth: we are assured that it took place, but we are not told why. In the gospel, however, the birth is seen as a vital link in 'salvation history', or *heilsgeschichte,* and is represented as the fulfilment of an ancient prophecy regarding the birth of Emmanuel — 'God is with us'. The idea was that this birth, so different from others, has as its object bringing God to man and man to God. This central notion of the Virgin Birth as a vital link in the salvation of man is beautifully illustrated in the Magnificat, the Virgin's Song, and in the Benedictus, the song sung by the father of John the Baptist, the herald of the Messiah (Luke 1). These are some of the absent associations which make one feel that there is a 'missing chapter' in the Qur'an. We miss the pathos of the crucifixion, the joyous resurrection and the inspiration which flows from the risen Christ.

The discussion may be taken a stage further by comparing what both the Qur'an and the gospels have to say about the works and mission of Jesus. In many respects the two accounts run on parallel lines. Both tell us that Jesus restored sight to the blind, cured the leper and raised the dead. The Qur'an even attributes to Jesus miracles which are not to be found in the gospels, describing him for instance as speaking in his cradle and, as a child, blowing on clay birds to make them take wing and fly.

The Qur'an designates these remarkable deeds as *bayyinat,* which may be translated as 'signs' or 'verifications'. Similarly, St John's Gospel refers to them as *semaia,* which is the Greek for 'signs'. But here the parallel ends. The profound significance of the miracles is to be found only in the synoptic gospels where they are shown to be, not so much signs of power, as of mercy, not displays of showmanship but works of compassion.

The account of a miracle in the gospels is often prefaced by some such phrase as 'He was moved by compassion', or, in modern English usage, 'His heart went out to them'. Very often, Jesus was moved to act by an anguished cry for help. A Roman centurion appeals to him on behalf of one of his boys who was lying paralysed; two blind men cry out, 'Son of David, have pity on us'. The father of a boy suffering from epileptic fits begs him to 'Have pity on my son'. Another father pleads for the life of his little girl.

The miracles were indeed signs, but they were signs that God had visited his people. This evocation of a prophet-*cum*-saviour is what we miss in the Qur'an. Muslim readers will appreciate this point since Muhammad's own mission is described as one of compassion: 'We have not sent thee, save as a mercy unto all beings' (Qur'an 21: 107; Arberry's translation).

The story of John the Baptist in the Qur'an gives rise to further puzzlement because, as in the case of Jesus, we are left with an enigma and a sense of incompleteness. Once again, the very name is changed from *Yohanna* in the gospels to the etymologically quite different *Yahya* of the Qur'an. This is no mere quibble since *Yohanna* means literally 'God has been gracious'. (The cognate Arabic root denotes the feeling of a mother yearning for her offspring.) But this sense is wholly absent from the Quranic name of Yahya for which commentators have found little or no meaning.

What has the Qur'an to say of John's mission? Very little. There are various respectful references to him, but they do not add up to a clear statement of what his mission was meant to be. Peace is invoked upon his birth, death and resurrection, as it is on Jesus', but there seems to be no suggestion of how he was connected with Jesus or of his role as a precursor. The only links, and they are tenuous, are first, that the accounts of the births of John and Jesus are found side by side in the chapter of the Qur'an entitled 'The House of 'Imran', and also in that entitled 'Mary'; and secondly, that Zacharia, the father of John the Baptist, is curiously credited in the Qur'an with having sheltered Mary during her pregnancy (Q. 3). But there is no hint in the Qur'an of the John of the gospels, the Messiah's herald, the voice crying in the wilderness, come to prepare men's hearts for the arrival of one mightier than he, who was to baptise not with water but with the holy spirit.

We cannot but appreciate what the Qur'an so eloquently tells us of both Jesus and John, but we can only wish there were more of it.

Beyond Politics

Among the many victories of Islam, both military and political, one of the earliest and perhaps most significant is often passed over. Muslim commentators tend to undervalue it if they do not misunderstand its importance altogether. It was a triumph of restraint and negotiation rather than of force, and thus presents militant Islam in a new light.

I refer to the al-Hudaybiya affair, a battle of wills between Muhammad and the Quraish on the frontiers of the holy precincts of Mecca. Muhammad, as we know, had left Mecca six years earlier as a fugitive. He was now attempting to return as a pilgrim and a worshipper. In his train were seven hundred of his followers, seventy sacrificial camels and several hundred other tribesmen eager for loot. Muhammad proclaimed that his aim was no more than a peaceful and devout visit to the Ka'aba.

But the Quraish, the dominant power in Mecca and among the surrounding tribes, were determined to deny him entry. They did not trust his peaceful intentions nor could they allow it to be said that Muhammad had forced an entry against their will. This would have meant a loss of face. So they donned their leopard skins, brought out their milch-camels and prepared for a long drawn-out contest.

The situation looked dangerous. It was rumoured that an envoy whom Muhammad had sent into Mecca had been killed. The Prophet summoned his men and asked them to pledge that they would fight for him to the death. But in both camps there seems to have been some embarrassment. At stake was prestige rather than material interests.

Pious folk among the Quraish felt that since Muhammad had come as a pilgrim — he was dressed as one and had brought sacrificial animals — it was wrong to keep him out. In the Muslim camp, the more zealous of Muhammad's followers were determined to force an entry at all costs. Not to enter Mecca would have damaged Muhammad's reputation or even cast doubt on his office as Prophet.

The Meccans finally advanced compromise terms. They suggested that Muhammad should forego entry this year but that if he were to return the following year he would be allowed to stay for three nights. In addition, there would be a ten-year truce in which the tribes would be free to join either side. To many Muslims the peace terms, with their stipulation of an immediate withdrawal, were intolerable. One influential voice, 'Umar's, expressed the bitterness they must all have felt:

Is he not God's apostle, and are we not Muslims, and
are they not polytheists? . . . Then why should we agree
to what is demeaning to our religion?[20]

But Muhammad accepted the terms and forced them on his reluctant followers. He did more than that. On profane ground, outside the sacred precincts, he went through the ritual of pilgrimage, shaving his head and slaughtering the sacrificial animals. In itself, this looked like an admission of failure.

But Ibn Ishaq, Muhammad's biographer, reviewing the incident a century after the Prophet's death, declared:

> No previous victory in Islam was greater than this. There was nothing but battle when men met; but when there was an armistice and war was abolished and men met in safety and consulted together none talked about Islam intelligently without entering it.[21]

Speaking of the al-Hudaybiya incident, the Qur'an contrasts the pride, savagery and unyielding spirit of the *Jahiliyya* with the restraint and calm of those possessed of reverence for God (*taqwah*).

What we admire about the al-Hudaybiya affair is the spirit of compromise displayed by the leaders of both camps. Is this not in fact the core of what Jesus stands for? 'Go first and make your peace with your brother,' he advised a would-be worshipper (Matt. 5: 24). He censures two fiery disciples who wanted to burn a Samaritan village to the ground because it had denied them entry (Luke 9: 54). 'Put up your sword,' he tells Peter at the moment of his capture (Matt. 28: 22). Indeed, one of his last words, addressed to the servant of the High Priest, was that no one had the right to strike a blow in retaliation for a word spoken amiss (John 18: 23). Was there anyone more deserving of the prophetic title, Prince of Peace?

Today, perhaps more than ever before, we are called to the negotiating table rather than the battlefield; we are called to talk rather than fight. The peace-makers, Jesus said, are God's own children.

Abraham

Consider the similarity between the following two passages from Bible and Qur'an:

> ... Abraham put his faith in God, and that faith was counted to him as righteousness; and elsewhere he is called 'God's friend'.
>
> [James 2: 23]

> 'And God took Abraham for a friend.'   [Q. 4: 125]

The Qur'an gives a graphic description of how Abraham found God. He first thought that he had found him in a star, but when it set he was disabused, saying: 'I love not those who set.' Later, when he finally experienced God, he smashed his father's idols and put his faith in God.

Muhammad recognised Abraham as the father of Ishmael and the ancestor of the Arabs. But it also dawned on Muhammad that there was something which could be called 'the religion of Abraham' – for Abraham, while not an idolater, was yet neither Jew nor Christian. He was a *Hanafite*: one who has yielded to God and become his friend.

For Muhammad this was a vast discovery. Without it, a pagan Arab repudiating idols and turning to God would have had to become a Jew and take upon himself the double yoke of the written and the oral law; or alternatively, to become a Christian and accept the gospel and with it the accretions which had come to be associated with it in the course of the centuries.

Far earlier, St. Paul had had a similar experience. After meeting with Jesus on the way to Damascus, he perceived in Abraham an exemplar who was justified by faith, justified by trust and surrender alone without recourse to the Law, because the Law did not yet exist. Even Abraham's own circumcision came later. Indeed, Abraham's justification was not mere aquittal since there was no law to break. In his case, justification could only mean that Abraham had become God's responsibility, that he had come to enjoy God's guidance and protection. On the basis of this analysis, St Paul advanced to the conclusion that we, although not physically related to Abraham, share his faith and therefore belong to him, since he was to be, according to God's promise, the father of many nations.

For St Paul, therefore, Abraham was justified not by keeping a set of commandments, but rather by having a trusting heart, cleansed and attuned to God. 'Abraham put his faith in God, and that faith was counted to him as righteousness' (Rom. 3: 4).

> Protestantism [says Adolf Harnack in his famous lectures on Christianity delivered at the University of Berlin] must be understood, first and foremost, by the contrast which it offers to Catholicism, and here there is a double direction which any estimate of it must take, first as *Reformation* and secondly as *Revolution* . . . religion was here brought back again to itself, in so far as the Gospel and the corresponding religious experience were put into the foreground and freed of all alien accretions . . . [religion] was reduced to its essential factors, to the Word of God and to faith.[22]

I should like to say only this in conclusion: I fear that Christians have not sufficiently appreciated Muhammad's discovery of Abraham; the polemical use to which it was later put does not detract from the greatness of the discovery. It is likewise significant that of all the titles which Abraham might have enjoyed, he was given but one — *khalil Allah*, 'the friend of God' — a title which tells us as much about Abraham's God as about Abraham himself. In the same manner Jesus tells his disciples: 'I call you servants no longer . . . I have called you friends ' (John 15: 15).

Notes

1. *Jawab ahl al-imam fi tafadul ay al-Qur'an*.
2. *Jawab ahl al-imam* . . . , p. 31.
3. *Jawab ahl al-imam* . . . , p. 30.
4. *Jawab ahl al-imam* . . . , p. 5.
5. *Jawab ahl al-imam* . . . , p. 123.
6. *Jawab ahl al-imam* . . . , p. 12.
7. *Jawab ahl al-imam* . . . , pp. 11-13.
8. *Itqan* II, p. 128.
9. *Life of al-Ghazali*, Journal of the American Oriental Society, vol. XX (1899), p. 72.
10. Algazel, *Tahafot al-Falasifat*, ed. Maurice Bouyges (Beyrouth, 1927), p. 349, n. 4, 5.
11. *Al-Madnun* (Cairo, 1309), H. p. 27; also *Ihya*, lv, 28 (Cairo, 1334) H.
12. *Al-Tahafut*, p. 3.
13. *Al-Tahafut*, p. 349.
14. *Al-Tahafut*, pp. 354-5.
15. *Al-Madnun*, pp. 26-8.
16. Mark 1: 27.
17. This is Professor Arberry's translation of *ummi*, which is usually rendered as 'illiterate'.
18. Al-Wahidi, *Asbab al-Nuzul* (Cairo 1959), p. 65.
19. Al-Wahidi, *Asbab al-Nuzul*, p. 35.
20. Ibn Ishaq, *Sirat Rasul Allah*, trans. A. Guillaume, p. 504.
21. Ibn Ishaq, *Sirat Rasul Allah*, p. 507.
22. Adolf Harnack, *What is Christianity?*, Trans. T.B. Saunders, 1904, p. 273.

INDEX

120

For Product Safety Concerns and Information please contact our EU
representative GPSR@taylorandfrancis.com
Taylor & Francis Verlag GmbH, Kaufingerstraße 24, 80331 München, Germany

www.ingramcontent.com/pod-product-compliance
Lightning Source LLC
Chambersburg PA
CBHW071136280326
41935CB00010B/1243

9 781032 946979